KT-489-000

50

THE
QUICK
AFTER-WORK
PASTA
COOKBOOK

THE
QUICK
AFTER-WORK
PASTA
COOKBOOK

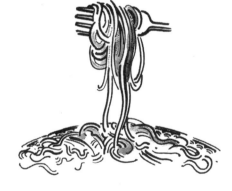

JUDY RIDGWAY

LONDON NEW YORK SYDNEY TORONTO

Copyright © 1993 Judy Ridgway

This edition published 1993
by BCA by arrangement with
Judy Piatkus (Publishers) Ltd, London W1

CN 3837

Printed in Great Britain

CONTENTS

INTRODUCTION

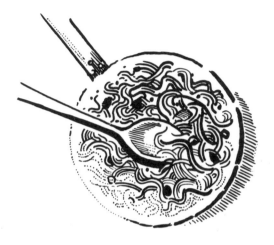

I was a bit of a late-comer to pasta but, like many converts, I am now quite fanatical about it and had no difficulty in coming up with the 100 or so recipes in this book. I rarely get bored with pasta because it is so versatile.

It is as delicious served with a simple vegetable sauce as with salmon or shellfish. It makes a quick and easy supper dish or it can form part of a grand dinner. Either way it never takes more than 15 minutes to cook and a good many sauces can be cooked in the same time.

My inspiration for these sauces is mainly Italian, probably because I first came to enjoy pasta as a result of visits to Italy. I can remember the first time I was presented with a mountain of genuine Italian pasta. We had escaped from our holiday hotel to a local restaurant in one of the villages above Amalfi in the Bay of Naples and pasta was the only choice. The food was cooked to order by the owner in a tiny kitchen at the back of the restaurant and the aromas were enticing. When the food arrived the waiter stood expectantly waiting for our praise. So, not wanting to disappoint him, I valiantly dug in. It was delicious and I was hooked!

I was struck, both on that holiday and on subsequent visits, by the way Italian cooks use punchy flavours with pasta. The pasta is not drowned in an indifferent sauce, as it is in the UK, but is well coated in a sauce of some intensity.

I have striven to capture this intensity of flavour in the sauces in this book and hope that I have succeeded. Luckily for today's home cook, long slow cooking is not the only way to distil the flavours of a dish; speedy reduction at high temperatures can work just as well.

Since that holiday in the Bay of Naples I have driven down the toe and heel of Italy, looked at olive groves in Abruzzo and studied wine in Tuscany and Piedmont. There have also been visits to the Italian lakes, holidays in Liguria and business meetings in Rome and Milan. On all these trips I have made notes on the classic sauces and asked chefs, friends and colleagues for their own favourite recipes.

Other ideas for sauces came from the Middle and Far East where egg noodles are almost as popular as pasta is in Italy. A recent visit to North America added some interesting variations on the Italian classics and I have also experimented with my own favourite ingredients to come up with the rest of the recipes.

The testing of the recipes for this book was much easier than I expected. Pasta is such a useful food for our modern lifestyle. It is very quick to cook and very versatile. It can form the basis for a meal in itself or it can be served, as in Italy, as one of two or three courses.

I found I could rush home from my office and prepare one of these dishes in a maximum of half an hour; many of them take even less time. If you only have 5 or 10 minutes turn to chapter One, Extra Quick Sauces.

The beauty of pasta dishes is that they are complete and require nothing else, but if you would like to serve a salad too, I have given some suggestions for combinations that work particularly well. Some people like to have bread to hand to mop up any extra sauce.

Pasta is also a convenient and enjoyable way of following the nutritionists' exhortations to eat more cereals. If you choose wholewheat pasta you will increase the fibre content of the meal even more. In addition, pasta contains the B complex vitamins and some minierals.

Many people believe that pasta is fattening. However it is not the pasta itself which sends the calories shooting up but the fat content of the sauce you toss it in. In fact you do not need large quantities of oil to dress pasta, a tablespoonful will do. Nor do you need to use too much fat in the sauce, and if you are tossing the pasta in a sauce it does not need to be dressed with oil as well. When cooked, a 125g (4oz) portion of pasta on its own yields about 150–180 calories.

I have kept a weather eye on the calorie content of my recipes and though this is not intended to be a book for slimmers there are recipes which they could use. Don't be put off by the cream or cheese recipes. The quantities are small when you consider that the recipes are all for four people or more.

It is usually accepted that people with any kind of wheat or gluten allergy are unable to eat pasta. I am pleased to say that this is no longer true. There are various types of pasta on sale in healthfood shops and specialist chemists which make use of rice, millet, barley and spelt. Of these I would recommend spelt, which can be eaten by people with a wheat allergy, and has a low gluten content. It does have quite a strong flavour of its own which overpowers some of the lighter sauces but it cooks exactly like wheat pasta and you can achieve the same kind of *al dente* texture. The others are terribly easy to overcook. The rice and millet spirals I tried went sticky within 3 minutes so they need very careful timing. However the flavour was not at all overpowering.

It is said that in Italy there are enough kinds of pasta to serve a different one every day. Elsewhere the choice may be slightly narrower but there are still a great many from which to choose. The big question these days is whether to buy fresh or dried pasta. Since the former seems to have become fashionable, traditional dried pasta manufacturers are offering ever more types of fresh pasta.

Personally I am not sure that fresh is best. Pasta, produced outside Italy, good as it is, just does not seem to have quite the same texture as pasta made in Italy and I wonder if quite the same high-quality hard wheat is used. Accordingly my form of one-upmanship is always to buy Italian pasta and, of course, outside Italy this means dried pasta. De Ceccho and La Terra e il Cielo are both very good brands to seek out.

Many people seem to think that fresh pasta is more authentic than dried. However this is just not true. A certain amount of special local-style pasta is still made in the home but it is only in Northern Italy that fresh pasta is offered for sale. Southern Italy is the home of dried pasta production and huge quantities are sold there.

Certain types of pasta lend themselves to particular sauces and so I have arranged this book by pasta style rather than by ingredients. Thus you will find all the long thin pastas like spaghetti and vermicelli in one chapter, and long flat pastas such as tagliatelle and fettucine in the next. These are followed by tubular pastas like penne and rigatoni and then by pasta shapes. Particularly quick pasta sauces are at the beginning.

There are no hard and fast rules about which sauce you should serve with what pasta and there is no pressing reason why you should not break with tradition and serve a Pesto Sauce with fusilli or a Carbonara Sauce with spaghetti. Very often the choice actually depends on what you have in stock! Nevertheless, I think long round pasta does work particularly well with oil-based sauces and that tubular pasta tastes better with a rich or thick sauce which will partially fill the hollows.

As well as being quick and easy to cook, dried pasta is also convenient to store. It will keep for a year or more in a dry cupboard and it is ready to cook straight from the pack. At any one time I usually have a couple of long pastas from which to choose, one variety of tubular pasta and some pasta shapes. Of course you don't need to have quite so many different pastas in your storecupboard – one will do. But if you are anything like me you will find that the more you get into pasta the more you want to experiment with all the different lengths, shapes and sizes!

COOKING PASTA

Pasta is very quick and easy to prepare; even the thickest of dried pastas cooks in 15 minutes. Fresh pasta cooks in 2 or 3 minutes. Overcooking is the only danger and it is a good idea to test the pasta 1–2 minutes before the cooking time is up.

Everyone has heard the phrase *al dente*, meaning 'firm to the bite', and this is essential for pasta. Overcooked pasta will be sticky and unpleasant.

QUANTITIES

The first step is to decide upon the quantity to be used. Appetites vary but here are my recommendations for pasta **for four people** in a variety of different serving situations:

	Dry	Fresh
Pasta as the basis of the dish	350g (12oz)	900g (2lb)
Pasta as a starter	175–225g (6–8oz)	450–600g (1–1¼lb)
Pasta as a side dish	225g (8oz)	600g (1¼lb)

Nearly all the recipes in this book are designed to serve four people as a main course or six people as a starter. In one or two cases smaller quantities than those given above are specified for a particular recipe; this is because the classic dish uses a lower ratio of pasta to sauce than usual. If you are cooking for a buffet party you can double the quantities but remember that as a general rule people do not eat quite so much standing up as they do sitting down.

COOKING METHOD

Whether it's fresh or dried, pasta needs plenty of boiling water. Allow at least 2.5 litres (4 pints) water for 225g (8oz) pasta. Too little water and the pasta will stick to itself and to the bottom of the pan.

1 Fill a large pan with salted water and add a teaspoon of olive oil. Bring the water to a fast boil.
2 Add the pasta to the boiling water fairly slowly so that the water does not go off the boil. Let long pieces of pasta curl round the pan as they soften, add tubular pasta and shapes gradually.
3 Cook the pasta uncovered at a steady boil, testing after about three-quarters of the cooking time. Overcooked pasta will be very sticky indeed.
4 When the pasta is cooked, drain in a colander and then toss at once with your chosen dressing or sauce. Do not leave even correctly cooked pasta to stand alone or it will start to stick together.

COOKING TIMES

Long thin dried pasta will take about 4–5 minutes, spaghetti and tagliatelle about 8–12 minutes and shapes anything up to 12–15 minutes. Different brands can vary quite considerably in their cooking times but they usually have cooking instructions on the pack. Follow these carefully and you will not go wrong.

Fresh pasta will take 2–3 minutes, though stuffed pasta like tortelloni may take a little longer. These will usually be cooked through when they rise and float on the top of the cooking water.

THE FINAL TOUCH

Freshy grated Parmesan is *the* traditional accompaniment, though this is not served with fish. Freshly ground black pepper is usually offered as well. Sprigs of fresh herbs are the modern garnish and, if carefully chosen to complement the sauce, can be very good indeed. Other accompaniments include chilli oil, freshly greated Pecorino cheese or a few drops of Tabasco sauce.

Some of the recipes include toasted nuts, pine kernels or seeds, either as a garnish or as part of the basic dish. Toasting brings out the flavour and the best way is to dry fry them in a hot frying pan until lightly browned. Keep them moving in the hot pan or they will burn.

· CHAPTER ONE ·

EXTRA QUICK SAUCES

Although all the recipes in this book are relatively quick to make there are times when you want to be able to get a meal onto the table in record time. The recipes in this section enable you to do just that. Bread and a simple side salad are optional accompaniments.

You can serve these sauces with any kind of pasta but if you do have a choice of pasta in your storecupboard try the oil- and butter-based sauces with spaghetti styles, the cream-based sauces with long flat pasta and the others with shapes or tubular pasta.

Ready-made stuffed pasta such as ravioli and tortelloni can be particularly quick to cook and usually only need the addition of a simple oil, butter or cream dressing, perhaps with some fresh herbs.

· *Oil-Based Sauces* ·

Olive oil is most certainly the first choice for a quick pasta dressing in Central and Southern Italy. The pasta is tossed in a full and fruity extra virgin oil and piled up in the serving dishes. Next comes the freshly grated Parmesan cheese and perhaps, but by no means as frequently as Italian restaurants outside Italy would have you believe, some freshly ground black pepper.

Extra Virgin Olive Oil

This is the top grade of olive oil. It is used as a condiment and flavouring in its own right. Ordinary olive oil is used for cooking when you do not particularly want the flavour of olives.

Olives for extra virgin oil are now all cold pressed in hydraulic presses and the oil is unrefined. Olives are grown all over Italy, Spain, Greece and Portugal and in Southern France. Each region produces oil with its own distinctive flavour. Some are quite mild and sweet. Others are more pungent, often with a peppery note to them. Choose your oil to match the other ingredients in the dish and use the same oil to dress a side salad.

Oil makes a very good dressing for pasta as it helps stop the pasta sticking together. It also carries the flavour of other ingredients well. The very simplest and quickest of dishes is made by gently heating lightly crushed cloves of garlic in a well-flavoured olive oil. The garlic should not burn. Strain the oil and use it to dress the pasta.

Dried and slightly crushed chillies are often added in Southern Italy where a piquant flavour is greatly appreciated. You could use chilli powder or a few drops of Tabasco instead. This dish is usually served without cheese but you might add a handful of freshly chopped parsley. The Italians maintain that this dish is a great hangover cure – if you eat it before you go to bed!

Other very quick ideas include tossing pasta in sun-dried tomato, artichoke or olive paste with additional olive oil and perhaps a few fried onion slices or some garlic.

The choice is not confined to olive oil. Nut oil, sesame oil and unrefined cold pressed sunflower oil also have definite flavours of their own and can be used with great effect to add interest to pasta dishes. Try tossing cooked pasta in almond oil and then serve with a sprinkling of toasted almond flakes. Or use a few drops of roasted sesame oil in a bland corn or sunflower oil and toss with pasta and fresh herbs.

ANCHOVY AND GARLIC SAUCE

This is a classic Italian sauce from the South where it is usually served with long round pasta. It has a punchy but not overpowering flavour. If you think the anchovies will be too strong for you, wash them under the cold tap before use or, for an even milder taste, soak in milk for a few minutes before draining, drying and chopping.

———— • ————

6 tablespoons olive oil
3 cloves garlic, peeled and crushed
1 × 50g (2oz) can anchovy fillets,
   drained and chopped

sufficient cooked pasta to serve 4 people
freshly ground black pepper

———— • ————

1 Heat the oil in a saucepan and fry the garlic for 1 minute.

2 Add the anchovies and continue cooking for 1–2 minutes over a medium heat until the fish breaks up to give a creamy sauce.

3 Toss the pasta in this sauce and serve with freshly ground black pepper.

Variation

Add a spoonful of capers or chopped black olives as you add the pasta.

ORIENTAL OYSTER MUSHROOM SAUCE

Oyster mushrooms cook in a flash, so you have to be careful not to overcook them. They also take up other flavours very well and this makes them a good base for extra quick sauces.

Do not serve cheese with this sauce, it simply doesn't work. Instead serve a salad of shredded Chinese leaves, beansprouts and grated carrot tossed in a simple vinaigrette flavoured with just a few drops of roasted sesame oil.

————— • —————

350g (12oz) oyster mushrooms
4 tablespoons olive oil
1 clove garlic (optional), peeled and crushed
1 large bunch fresh chives, chopped

1 tablespoon soy sauce
4 tablespoons orange juice
a little grated orange rind
pinch of five spice powder
sufficient cooked pasta to serve 4 people

————— • —————

1 Roughly chop the mushrooms just before starting to cook.

2 Heat the oil in a large frying pan and gently fry the garlic, if using, and half the chives for 1 minute.

3 Add the soy sauce, orange juice and orange rind and bring to the boil. Continue cooking for 2–3 minutes to reduce a little.

4 Add the five spice powder and oyster mushrooms and toss all together over a medium heat for about 1 minute. Spoon over the pasta, sprinkle with the remaining chives and serve at once.

Variations

1 Add the sliced peel from 3 kumquats with the oranges.

2 Instead of five spice powder, add 1 teaspoon roasted sesame oil and sprinkle with toasted sesame seeds.

LIGURIAN SAUCE

This receipe uses similar ingredients to Pesto Sauce, the Ligurian speciality, but is even quicker to make. Serve with a simple tomato salad.

———— • ————

4 tablespoons olive oil
50g (2oz) pine kernels, toasted (see page xi)
a pinch of salt
2–3 tablespoons freshly chopped basil leaves

1–2 cloves garlic, peeled and finely chopped
sufficient cooked pasta to serve 4 people
freshly grated Parmesan cheese

———— • ————

1 Heat the oil in a large pan and add all the remaining ingredients except the pasta and cheese. Cook for 1 minute.

2 Toss the pasta in the mixture and serve with Parmesan.

PIMENTO AND SALAMI SAUCE

Pimento paste is on sale in specialist delicatessen shops and Italian grocers. It is made from sweet peppers and is not at all hot. Serve with a salad of lettuce and watercress.

———— • ————

sufficient cooked pasta to serve 4 people
4 tablespoons olive oil, warmed
1 small jar pimento paste

75g (3oz) salami, diced
20 very large salted capers, soaked in water and drained

———— • ————

1 Toss the pasta in the oil and add the pimento paste and salami.

2 Toss again and serve sprinkled with capers.

SYRIAN SAUCE

This Middle Eastern sauce is usually used with a tubular pasta such as macaroni. It is very aromatic and goes well with kebabs.

————— • —————

4 tablespoons olive oil
1 onion, peeled and finely chopped
2 cloves garlic, peeled and finely chopped
2 tablespoons freshly chopped parsley
1 teaspoon freshly chopped mint

1/4 teaspoon ground cinnamon
salt and freshly ground black pepper
sufficient cooked pasta to serve 4 people
  as a starter or side dish
a few sprigs of fresh parsley

————— • —————

1 Heat the oil in a saucepan and fry the onion and garlic until they are golden brown.

2 Stir in all the other ingredients, including the pasta. Toss well together and serve garnished with sprigs of fresh parsley.

Variation

Garnish with raisins and freshly toasted pine kernels (see page xi).

· *Butter-Based Sauces* ·

Butter is used in Northern Italy but rarely in Central and Southern Italy. In Milan long pasta tossed in melted butter and grated Parmesan is sometimes known as 'Inglese' or English sauce. Add a little sage and black pepper for a very classic dressing for plain or stuffed pasta. Nutmeg, too, marries very well with butter.

HAM AND CHEESE SAUCE

Very simple, easily available ingredients make this a good standby on busy evenings. The sauce will probably be ready before the pasta! So while you're waiting, prepare a simple green salad to accompany it.

——— · ———

75g (3oz) unsalted butter
75g (3oz) cooked ham, diced
125g (4oz) freshly grated Parmesan
  cheese

sufficient cooked pasta to serve 4 people
salt and freshly ground black pepper

——— · ———

1 Melt the butter in a saucepan and toss in the ham and cheese.

2 Add the pasta to the pan, season and toss all together.

Variation

Omit the ham and use toasted pine kernels (see page xi) for texture instead.

HUNGARIAN SAUCE

Toasted poppy seeds are very popular in Hungary where they are used in all kinds of savoury dishes as well as on cakes and bread. Here they add a crunchy texture as well as an unusual flavour.

——— • ———

75g (3oz) butter

2 tablespoons poppy seeds, toasted (see page xi)

sufficient cooked pasta to serve 4 people

freshly grated Parmesan cheese

——— • ———

1 Melt the butter in a large saucepan. Add the poppy seeds and pasta and toss well together.

2 Serve with freshly grated Parmesan cheese.

Variation

Reduce the quantity of butter and add some cream.

QUICK PRAWN SAUCE

I sometimes use Morecambe Bay potted shrimps for this recipe because of their excellent flavour. But this can be a bit expensive for 4 people.

——— • ———

125g (4oz) unsalted butter

175g (6oz) cooked peeled prawns

freshly ground black pepper

a generous sprinkling of grated nutmeg

sufficient cooked pasta to serve 4 people

freshly chopped parsley

——— • ———

1 Melt the butter in a large saucepan and add the prawns, pepper and nutmeg.

2 Toss with the pasta and serve at once, sprinkled with freshly chopped parsley.

· *Cream-Based Sauces* ·

Cream and pasta make a great combination. All kinds of simple flavourings can be added to the cream to make a very quick sauce indeed. If you feel that cream on its own is too rich for you, combine it with a good stock and boil fast to thicken. Then throw in some diced artichoke bases, fresh peas, or shredded spinach and you have a sauce fit for a dinner party.

Yoghurt can be used in place of some or all of the cream but it will need to be stabilised with a little cornflour or potato flour. The flavour will, of course, be quite different. Use strained Greek yoghurt for a creamier texture.

QUICK CREAM AND HERB SAUCE

Almost any fresh herbs can be used in this very simple sauce. Try parsley, chervil or dill in these quantities or slightly less tarragon, sorrel or fennel. Good combinations are parsley and tarragon, and sorrel with a pinch of dried thyme. Serve with a lamb's lettuce or corn lettuce salad.

——— · ———

250ml (8fl oz) double cream
2 tablespoons strong vegetable or chicken stock

salt and freshly ground black pepper
4–5 tablespoons freshly chopped herbs
sufficient cooked pasta to serve 4 people

——— · ———

1 Place the cream, stock and seasoning in a saucepan and bring to the boil.

2 After about 3 minutes add the chopped herbs and continue cooking over a fairly high heat.

3 When the sauce thickens, taste and adjust the seasoning. Simply pour over the pasta, toss and serve.

GREEN PEPPERCORN SAUCE

I usually make this sauce with fresh green peppercorns which are very aromatic and spicy; if you use bottled peppercorns you may need to add more. Fresh peppercorns blacken very quickly so use as soon after purchase as possible.

———— • ————

25g (1oz) fresh green peppercorns or
  35g (1½oz) bottled green peppercorns
25g (1oz) butter

1 clove garlic, peeled and crushed
250ml (8fl oz) double cream
sufficient cooked pasta to serve 4 people

———— • ————

1 Strip the fresh peppercorns from their stalks, or rinse bottled peppercorns.

2 Gently fry the peppercorns in the butter for 5–6 minutes, until they begin to pop. Try not to burn the butter.

3 Stir in the garlic, cook for 1 minute and add the cream. Bring to the boil and cook for a further 2–3 minutes. Toss with the pasta and serve at once.

RED ONION SAUCE

The red onions add a pretty pink colour to this well-flavoured sauce from Northern Italy. Serve with all kinds of long pasta and a salad of Lollo Rosso to echo the colours.

———— • ————

50g (2oz) butter
2 cloves garlic, peeled and finely chopped
1 large red onion, peeled and finely chopped
a large bunch of broadleaf parsley, roughly chopped

a pinch of dried marjoram
salt and freshly ground black pepper
150ml (¼ pint) double cream
sufficient cooked pasta to serve 4 people
freshly grated Parmesan cheese

———— • ————

1 Melt the butter in a deep pan and gently fry the garlic and onion for 3–4 minutes. Do not allow the onion to burn.

2 Add the herbs, seasoning and cream and bring to the boil. Simmer for 2–3 minutes and add the pasta.

3 Toss and serve with grated Parmesan on the side.

CREAMED PROSCIUTTO SAUCE

This rich sauce is excellent with long flat pasta or with tubular pasta. It is much easier to chop the prosciutto if you ask the shop assistant to cut it in one thick piece rather than in the more usual thin slices.

———— • ————

50g (2oz) butter
150ml (¼ pint) double cream
50g (2oz) prosciutto or Parma ham, very finely chopped

grated nutmeg
salt and freshly ground black pepper
75g (3oz) freshly grated Parmesan cheese
sufficient cooked pasta to serve 4 people

———— • ————

1 Melt the butter in a very large saucepan and pour in the cream. Bring the mixture to the boil and cook for 1 minute.

2 Add the prosciutto to the pan with the nutmeg and seasoning. Check the balance of flavours before adding the cheese.

3 Toss the pasta in the sauce and serve at once with more black pepper and Parmesan on the side.

GORGONZOLA CREAM SAUCE

This Italian blue cheese has a creamy texture and tastes very tangy. It can be used to make quite simple but well-flavoured sauces. The more cheese you add, the stronger the flavour.

———— • ————

100ml (4fl oz) double cream
25g (1oz) butter
175g (6oz) Gorgonzola cheese, cut into pieces

salt and freshly ground black pepper
a good pinch of grated nutmeg
sufficient cooked pasta to serve 4 people

———— • ————

1 Place all the ingredients except the pasta in a saucepan and bring to the boil over a gentle heat.

2 As soon as the mixture boils remove from the heat and pour over the pasta. Toss and serve.

Variations

1 For an even richer flavour, add 50ml (2fl oz) dry vermouth to 150ml (¼ pint) cream and omit the butter.

2 Fry a crushed clove of garlic and some sprigs of sage in the butter before beating into the cheese and cream. Discard the sage leaves.

DOLCELATTE AND WALNUT SAUCE

Dolcelatte is a milder, creamier version of Gorgonzola. The same effect can be achieved by using Gorgonzola with mascarpone. Serve with a delicate salad of lamb's lettuce dressed with walnut oil.

———— • ————

175g (6oz) Dolcelatte cheese
100ml (4fl oz) double cream
salt and freshly ground black pepper

sufficient cooked pasta to serve 4 people
50g (2oz) walnuts, chopped

———— • ————

1 Melt the cheese in the cream over a low heat and bring to the boil. Season to taste.

2 Toss the pasta in the sauce with the walnuts and serve at once.

Variation

Use soft goat's cheese or Boursin for a change of flavour.

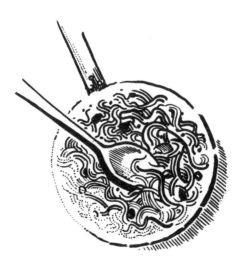

CREAMED FETA AND OLIVE SAUCE

Various soft cheeses can be used in this way. Try Mozzarella with tubular pasta or Brie with long thin pasta like vermicelli or linguine. Serve as a starter with a sliced tomato and onion salad.

————— • —————

250ml (8fl oz) double cream
125g (4oz) Feta cheese, crumbled
12 black olives, stoned and chopped
leaves from 4 large sprigs of basil, roughly torn

freshly ground black pepper
sufficient cooked pasta to serve 4 as a starter

————— • —————

1 Heat the cream in a saucepan and bring to the boil. Cook for a few minutes to reduce.

2 Add the Feta cheese and continue cooking, stirring all the time until the Feta has partially melted.

3 Stir in all the remaining ingredients. Toss well together and serve with more freshly ground black pepper.

RICOTTA AND TOMATO SAUCE

Any kind of ricotta can be used for this recipe. You can also quite successfully substitute cottage cheese. A side salad of baby spinach leaves or watercress makes the ideal accompaniment.

————— • —————

150ml (¼ pint) double cream
150g (5oz) ricotta or cottage cheese, crumbled

3 ripe tomatoes, seeded and chopped
salt and freshly ground black pepper
sufficient cooked pasta to serve 4 people

————— • —————

1 Gently heat the cream in a large saucepan. Add the cheese and continue cooking for 2 minutes until very hot.

2 Stir in the tomatoes and seasonings. Add the pasta and toss all together. Serve with more freshly ground black pepper.

Variation

Substitute 75g (3oz) coarsely chopped walnuts for the tomatoes and add mascarpone instead of the cream.

PRAWN AND GARLIC SAUCE

You can use any kind of garlic-flavoured cheese for this well-flavoured quickie. Boursin, Bressot or garlic roulade all work well. Serve with long flat pasta for the best results.

———— • ————

1 × 175g (6oz) Boursin cheese   *freshly ground black pepper*
3 tablespoons double cream   *sufficient cooked pasta to serve 4 people*
125g (4oz) cooked and peeled prawns *freshly chopped parsley*

———— • ————

1 Heat the cheese in a small saucepan with the cream. Stir until all the cheese has melted. Bring to the boil and remove from the heat.

2 Stir in the prawns and pepper. Toss together and pour over the pasta. Serve sprinkled with the chopped parsley.

VESUVIO SAUCE

This opulent recipe is the house speciality of Vesuvio, an Italian restaurant on the Croisette in Cannes. During the summer there are usually queues of people waiting to get in. You can economise by buying smoked salmon trimmings but whole slices look better. Lightly steamed mangetout make a good accompaniment.

—————— • ——————

250ml (8fl oz) double cream
25g (1oz) butter
salt

12–14 whole black peppercorns
125g (4oz) smoked salmon
sufficient cooked pasta to serve 4 people

—————— • ——————

1 Put the cream, butter and salt into a large saucepan and bring to the boil. Simmer fast for 5 minutes, stirring from time to time.

2 Meanwhile dry fry the black peppercorns or toast them under the grill.

3 Cut the smoked salmon into 5cm (2in) strips and add to the cream. Stir and add the pasta.

4 Toss and serve, garnished with the toasted peppercorns.

· *Egg-Based Sauces* ·

If you add beaten egg to piping hot pasta it will cook in the residual heat. If the pasta has cooled too much, a touch of heat to the base of the pan will do the trick. Work as fast as you can, tossing the mixture so that the egg coats all the strands. If you take too long over this all the egg will sink to the base of the pan and set there.

EGG AND CAPER SAUCE

This recipe comes from a Canadian friend living in Rome. She uses this mixture with fairly thin pasta such as trenette or linguine but you could also use fettucine.

———— · ————

3 eggs, beaten
125g (4oz) Pecorino Romano cheese, finely grated
1 tablespoon capers, drained

salt and freshly ground black pepper
25g (1oz) butter
sufficient cooked pasta to serve 4 people

———— · ————

1 Mix the eggs with half the cheese, all the capers and some seasoning and beat well together.

2 Heat the butter in a large saucepan and add the pasta.

3 Pour the egg and cheese mixture over the top. Toss well together. Serve with more black pepper and the rest of the Pecorino.

EGG AND TARRAGON SAUCE

Egg and tarragon is an excellent combination but you can use parsley, dill or chervil if tarragon is not to hand. Serve with a radicchio salad dressed with extra virgin olive oil.

———— • ————

3 eggs, beaten
125g (4oz) Parmesan cheese, finely grated
salt and freshly ground black pepper
1 tablespoon freshly chopped tarragon

2–3 spring onions, finely chopped
25g (1oz) butter
sufficient cooked long pasta to serve 4 people

———— • ————

1 Mix the eggs with half the cheese, seasoning, tarragon and spring onion and beat well together.

2 Heat the butter in a large saucepan and add the pasta.

3 Pour the egg and cheese mixture over the top and toss well together. Serve with more black pepper and the rest of the Parmesan.

EGG AND ARTICHOKE SAUCE

Artichoke paste can be bought in jars from specialist stockists of Italian foods. Once opened it can be kept in the fridge for a week or so.

———— • ————

3 eggs, beaten
2 tablespoons artichoke pasta
50g (2oz) ricotta cheese, crumbled
salt and freshly ground black pepper

25g (1oz) butter
sufficient cooked long pasta to serve 4 people

———— • ————

1 Mix the eggs with the artichoke paste, cheese and seasoning. Beat well.

2 Heat the butter in a large saucepan and add the pasta.

3 Pour the egg and artichoke mixture over the top. Toss well together. Serve with more black pepper.

LONG ROUND PASTA

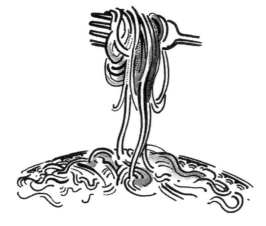

L ong round pasta in the form of spaghetti is without doubt the best-known style of pasta outside Italy. It is very versatile and can be served with almost any kind of sauce. Certainly all the quick sauces in Chapter 1 will work well with it. However, light oil-based sauces are particularly good because they allow the strands to remain separate and slippery.

All the types of long round pasta listed below are available dried and quite a few of them are available fresh. Many are on sale in wholewheat versions but these are not Italian in origin. Bigoli (see below) is the only pasta traditionally made with wholemeal flour in Italy.

You can also buy brands of spaghetti flavoured with tomato, mushrooms and even truffles but I find them rather bitter and prefer to add these flavours by way of the sauce.

For cooking instructions, see page xi.

SPAGHETTI

There is some variation in the length of this long and fairly thin round pasta. I remember when shops in the UK only sold spaghetti which was at least 40cm (14–16in) long but now there seems to be a trend towards shorter lengths of 25cm (10in) or 30cm (12in).

SPAGHETTINI

This is a thinner version of medium-length spaghetti. It is often used for fish-based or seafood sauces.

VERMICELLI

This is the name used for spaghettini in Southern Italy. However some producers make an even finer, threadlike pasta which they call vermicelli but which is more like capelli d'angelo.

CAPELLI D'ANGELO

'Angel hair' is the English translation for this extremely thin threadlike pasta. It is usually served with a very light sauce or in soup.

TONNARELLI

This is a home-made square spaghetti. In Abruzzo it is known as *maccheroni alla chitarra*. In practice it is interchangeable with normal spaghetti.

BIGOLI

Originating in the region around Venice, this is the only traditional Italian pasta made with wholemeal flour. It is long and thick and the dough is bound with eggs, often duck eggs.

SUN-DRIED TOMATO AND RED PEPPER SAUCE

Mediterranean cooks have found that grilling peppers seems to make them sweeter and even more aromatic. I also think that the slightly charred taste of any remaining bits of skin adds to the flavour. This was certainly the case when I first came across this dish in a small inn on the outskirts of Perugia in Central Italy. We started our evening meal with a hearty bean and vegetable soup. The pasta was accompanied by a green salad tossed in the local olive oil.

———— • ————

25g (1oz) sun-dried tomatoes
2–3 red peppers depending on size, quartered and seeded
4 tablespoons extra virgin olive oil

1 onion, peeled and sliced
salt and freshly ground black pepper
sufficient cooked pasta to serve 4 people
matured Pecorino cheese, grated

———— • ————

1 Soak the sun-dried tomatoes in boiling water to soften them if they are dry and cut into thin strips.

2 Place the peppers skin side up under the grill and cook until they are well charred. Remove from the heat and leave to stand for 10 minutes. Peel and cut into strips.

3 Heat the oil in a frying pan and gently fry the onion until it starts to brown. Add the strips of tomato, red pepper and seasoning. Toss well together over a medium heat.

4 Drain the pasta and place on 4 serving plates. Top with the tomato and pepper mixture, and serve with more olive oil and Pecorino cheese.

Sun-Dried Tomatoes

You can buy these strongly flavoured dried tomatoes loose or packed in oil. The former need to be soaked in boiling water before use. Sun-dried tomatoes can also be bought puréed and a teaspoonful of this paste will jazz up all kinds of tomato and meat-based sauces.

TOMATO SAUCE

Wherever you go in Italy you can be sure that the chefs and cooks will offer you their own version of Tomato Sauce (Salsa di Pomodoro). As well as the ripest tomatoes, fresh herbs, lemon zest and chilli peppers are used to add even more flavour. More substantial sauces use olives, tuna or prosciutto (raw cured ham). The sunshine of Italy seems to be distilled into their tomatoes so, if you can, use Italian plum tomatoes or add a little concentrated tomato purée.

SIMPLE TOMATO SAUCE FROM NAPLES

In the eighteenth century Naples became the Italian home of tomatoes from the New World. The cooks did not bother to peel them, but they were usually seeded and coarsely chopped. It is only in relatively recent times that tomatoes have been peeled for a Tomato Sauce so the choice is yours.

——————— • ———————

2 cloves garlic, peeled and crushed
4 tablespoons olive oil
900g (2lb) really ripe tomatoes, coarsely
   chopped

a pinch of sugar
salt and freshly ground black pepper
sufficient cooked pasta to serve 4 people
freshly grated Parmesan cheese

——————— • ———————

1 Gently fry the garlic in olive oil in the base of a deep pan. Add the tomatoes after 1–2 minutes, together with the sugar and seasonings.

2 Bring to the boil and cook over a medium heat for 10–15 minutes, stirring fairly often. The tomatoes should cook down to a thick sauce. You can use the sauce as it is or purée in a blender.

3 Spoon the sauce over the pasta or toss together and serve with freshly grated Parmesan.

Variations

1 Add 1 tablespoon tomato purée if the tomatoes are not as ripe as they might be or use 2 × 600g (1¼lb) cans of tomatoes instead. With the latter, continue cooking until all the liquid has evaporated.

2 Add 1 small peeled and finely chopped onion or 1 seeded and finely chopped green (or red) chilli pepper with the garlic.

3 Add dried thyme, bayleaf or oregano with the tomatoes.

Tuscan Tomato and Basil Sauce

The carrot gives an added sweetness to this traditionally robust sauce from Tuscany. Serve with a green salad dressed with ewe's or goat's milk ricotta and lemon juice.

———— • ————

*700g (1½lb) ripe tomatoes
 or 2 × 400g (14oz) cans tomatoes
1 small carrot, peeled and grated
salt and freshly ground black pepper*

*leaves from 5–6 sprigs of basil, roughly
 chopped
sufficient cooked pasta to serve 4 people
freshly grated Parmesan cheese*

———— • ————

1 Place the fresh or canned tomatoes in a saucepan and add the carrot and seasonings.

2 Bring to the boil, cover and cook over a medium heat for 15–20 minutes until fairly thick.

3 Purée in a blender. Add the basil and spoon over the pasta. Serve with freshly grated Parmesan.

Variations

1 Add half a finely chopped small onion with the grated carrot.

2 Instead of basil, flavour with a little grated lemon rind and the juice of 1 small orange.

CLASSIC TOMATO SAUCE

This classic sauce, which is made all over Italy, does not really take very much longer to make but it does have a much more complex flavour than the simple sauces. Make in double or treble quantities and freeze for future use. Serve as it is or flavour with fresh or dried herbs.

———————— • ————————

1 small onion, peeled and finely chopped
3 tablespoons olive oil
1 small carrot, peeled and finely chopped
2 sticks celery, trimmed and finely chopped

500ml (18fl oz) passato di pomodoro or 1 × 600g (1¼lb) can chopped tomatoes
salt and freshly ground black pepper
sufficient cooked pasta to serve 4 people
freshly grated Parmesan cheese

———————— • ————————

1 Gently fry the onion in the olive oil for about 1 minute. Add the carrot and celery and continue to fry gently for another 2 minutes. Do not allow the vegetables to brown.

2 Add the passato or chopped tomatoes and seasoning and bring to the boil. Simmer for 20–30 minutes until the sauce has thickened.

3 Purée in a blender.

4 Spoon over the pasta and serve with freshly grated Parmesan.

Passato

Passato di pomodoro simply consists of mashed or strained tomatoes. Passato is much more liquid than tomato purée which is too thick and concentrated to use on its own. If passato is unavailable you can use canned chopped tomatoes instead.

MUSHROOM SAUCE

Like Tomato Sauce, this thick paste of cooked mushrooms will be found in every Italian cook's repertoire. It is particularly useful because any kind of mushroom can be used, even rather tired button mushrooms!

I often make double or treble quantities and keep batches in the freezer to use in more substantial sauces, such as Variation 2 (below).

——————— • ———————

1–2 large cloves garlic to taste, peeled and crushed
6–7 tablespoons olive oil or 75g (3oz) butter

350g (12oz) mushrooms, minced or very finely chopped
salt and freshly ground black pepper
a little double cream (optional)
sufficient cooked pasta to serve 4 people

——————— • ———————

1 Gently fry the garlic in the oil (or butter) until it starts to colour.

2 Add the mushrooms and seasoning. Cook slowly until the mixture softens and darkens; this may take up to 15 minutes. Take care that it does not burn.

3 Discard any liquid and add a little more oil or just enough double cream to make a thick sauce. Add the pasta and toss together.

Variations

1 Cover 8–15g (¼–½oz) dried mushrooms with boiling water and leave to stand for 20 minutes. Mince with the fresh mushrooms. This will give ordinary button mushrooms a lift.
2 Prepare 4 Italian sausages as directed on page 85, skin and crumble the cooked meat. Mix with the Mushroom Sauce, 2 tablespoons freshly chopped parsley and a little more olive oil.

CREAM AND HERB SAUCE

A recipe for a simple Cream and Herb Sauce is given in the Extra Quick Sauces chapter on page 9. This version requires a little more effort but it is more than repaid by the added subtlety of flavour. Almost any kind of herb can be used. In addition to the more obvious herbs, try watercress, fennel, lemon balm or chervil. This sauce is delicious with delicate capelli d'angelo pasta. Follow it with some fresh pears and almonds.

———— • ————

75ml (3fl oz) well-flavoured vegetable *a pinch of cayenne pepper*
* or chicken stock* *a pinch of grated nutmeg*
150ml (¼ pint) double cream *125g (4oz) freshly grated Parmesan*
50g (2oz) butter, cut into pieces * cheese*
salt and freshly ground black pepper *4 tablespoons freshly chopped herbs*
sufficient cooked pasta to serve 4 people

———— • ————

1 Place the stock and cream in a pan and bring to the boil. Simmer over a medium heat to reduce.

2 After 6–7 minutes, start beating in pieces of butter with a wooden spoon. When all the butter has been incorporated, stir in the seasonings, cayenne and nutmeg.

3 Next add half the cheese, the herbs and the pasta. Toss well together and serve with the rest of the Parmesan sprinkled over the top.

BROCCOLI AND PINE KERNEL SAUCE

I came across this unusual sauce on a motoring holiday along the Italian coast south of Naples. We stopped off for a leisurely four-course lunch in a restaurant in the main square at Salerno and this dish was served as our second course. It is both extremely quick to make and attractive to look at. The flavours and textures are good too.

—————— • ——————

4 tablespoons olive oil
2 cloves garlic, peeled and crushed
125g (4oz) breadcrumbs
salt and freshly ground black pepper
350g (12oz) broccoli, cut into florets

sufficient cooked pasta to serve 4 people
2 tablespoons pine kernels, toasted (see
  page xi)
freshly grated Parmesan cheese

—————— • ——————

1 Heat the oil in a large frying pan and fry the garlic for 1 minute. Add the breadcrumbs and seasoning and fry until crisp and golden.

2 Cook the broccoli in a little salted boiling water or steam until just tender. Do not allow it to overcook or it will go soggy.

3 Place a portion of pasta on each plate and sprinkle on the breadcrumbs. Pile the broccoli in the centre and sprinkle with the toasted pine kernels.

4 Serve with extra virgin olive oil and freshly grated Parmesan cheese.

Variations

1 Add 2 tablespoons sesame seeds to the breadcrumbs and leave out the garlic and pine kernels. Add a little roasted sesame oil to some more olive oil and serve on the side.

2 Add 1 × 50g (2oz) can anchovies, drained and chopped, to the breadcrumb mixture and leave out the garlic and Parmesan cheese.

LEBANESE LENTIL SAUCE

I've never really thought of the Middle East as a pasta-eating area but a Lebanese friend of mine often serves noodles with her main course dishes. Lentils, on the other hand, are very much a part of the Lebanese tradition and are often served mixed with rice. She tells me that this recipe is supposed to be older than Marco Polo, but where the pasta came from in those days is anybody's guess.

———— • ————

125g (4oz) whole green lentils, washed
4 tablespoons olive oil
1 large onion, peeled and finely chopped
1 large clove garlic, peeled and finely chopped
salt and freshly ground black pepper

2 tablespoons freshly chopped coriander leaves
sufficient cooked pasta to serve 4 people
a few sprigs of fresh coriander

———— • ————

1 Cover the lentils with plenty of water and bring to the boil. Simmer for 20–25 minutes until just tender. Do not allow them to overcook and go mushy.

2 Heat the oil in another pan and fry the onion and garlic until they are golden brown. Add the drained lentils, seasonings and coriander and mix carefully together.

3 Add a little olive oil to the pasta and spoon on the lentil sauce. Garnish with sprigs of fresh coriander.

SICILIAN PEPPER SAUCE

Capers and olives are typical ingredients in the food of this sun-drenched island. They are used here with succulent sweet peppers and onions. I like to serve this sauce with long thin pasta such as vermicelli or capelli d'angelo, and mop up the juices with a warm ciabatta roll. The flavour improves with keeping, so make double quantities and use again later.

——— • ———

4 large peppers of mixed colours, quartered and seeded
2 large onions, peeled and sliced
2 cloves garlic, peeled and chopped
5 tablespoons extra virgin olive oil
1 tablespoon red wine vinegar
1 teaspoon tomato purée

6 large green olives, stoned and chopped
1 tablespoon capers, drained and washed
salt and freshly ground black pepper
a pinch of dried oregano
sufficient cooked pasta to serve 4 people
freshly grated Parmesan cheese

——— • ———

1 Grill the peppers or char over an open flame. Peel and cut into strips.

2 Fry the onion and garlic in the olive oil for 4–5 minutes until lightly browned.

3 Add all the remaining sauce ingredients, with 2 tablespoons water, and bring to the boil. Cook over a medium heat for 10 minutes, stirring from time to time. Spoon onto the pasta and serve with freshly grated Parmesan.

Variations

1 Add 3–4 anchovy fillets, well chopped, or 2 teaspoons anchovy pâté (see page 33). Serve with chopped parsley rather than Parmesan.

2 Use vinegar aged with herbs or orange peel for extra flavour.

PROVENÇAL SAUCE

In some ways the food of Provence is almost as Italian as Italy itself. Traditional dishes such as Pissaladiere and Soupe au Pistou with its garlic and basil sauce are very similar to Italian specialities like Pizza and Pesto Sauce. Indeed at one time the coastal areas of Provence, from Monte Carlo in the East to Toulon in the West, were all part of the Italian province of Liguria.

The Italian influences are still very strong. This is a typical Provence-style sauce for pasta. It has a tendency to splash when it is boiling fast so use a very deep pan, but do not cover with a lid. Being oil-based, this sauce goes well with any kind of long pasta but I like it particularly with vermicelli.

———— • ————

2 large cloves garlic, peeled and chopped
1 medium onion, peeled and finely chopped
2 tablespoons olive oil
1 × 400g (14oz) can tomatoes
25g (1oz) Nice or small black olives

1 heaped teaspoon large Italian capers
salt and freshly ground black pepper
leaves from 2 large sprigs basil, roughly torn
sufficient cooked pasta to serve 4 people

———— • ————

1 Fry the garlic and onion in the oil for 4–5 minutes until lightly browned.

2 Add the tomatoes, olives, capers and seasonings and bring to the boil. Boil fast for 15 minutes, stirring every so often to stop the sauce sticking to the pan.

3 Just before serving add the basil and toss with the pasta.

ASPARAGUS TIPS WITH LEMON GRASS

Pasta, so they say, was invented in the East so I have combined some of the flavours of Thai and Malaysian cooking with fresh spring vegetables to make a very attractive dish. Try to keep the vegetables just slightly crunchy and arrange the plates with care. Crunchy deep-fried prawns make a wonderful starter to this meal.

———————— • ————————

3 short sticks lemon grass
3 cloves garlic, peeled and halved
2 small pieces fresh root ginger, peeled
6 tablespoons peanut oil
12 baby sweetcorn, cut in half lengthways
450g (1lb) asparagus, trimmed and cut into lengths

125g (4oz) mangetout, trimmed and cut in half lengthways
juice of 2 oranges
¼ teaspoon ground coriander
sufficient cooked pasta to serve 4 people
4 tablespoons desiccated coconut, toasted under a hot grill

———————— • ————————

1 Gently fry the lemon grass, garlic and root ginger in the oil for 2–3 minutes, taking care not to let the oil get too hot. Take the flavourings out of the oil with a slotted spoon and discard.

2 Boil the baby sweetcorn in salted water for about 5 minutes.

3 Reheat the flavoured oil and add the baby sweetcorn, together with the asparagus and mangetout. Toss all the vegetables until they are well coated. Add the orange juice and coriander and bring to the boil. Simmer for 5 minutes until the asparagus is just tender.

4 Add the pasta and toss well together.

5 Spoon onto 4 plates, pouring the juices over the top, and sprinkle with the toasted coconut.

Variations

1 Replace the basil with a mixture of fresh parsley and tarragon.

2 Replace the basil with 2 teaspoons anchovy pâté (see page 33). The result is astonishingly different.

ITALIAN GREEN HERB SAUCE

Salsa Verde

This pretty green sauce and its more piquant cousin (see opposite) do not need cooking but they can be very gently heated to stop the pasta going cold too quickly. Take care not to overheat them. They can both be made in a food processor or blender. The flavour remains as good but the texture disappears, leaving a fairly smooth and creamy sauce.

Both sauces improve with keeping. I often make double quantities and store half in the fridge to use later in the week. They are both served as starters, as it is difficult to keep larger quantities of pasta hot.

---

a mixed bunch of fresh parsley and basil
2 small sticks celery, trimmed and chopped
1/2 small onion, peeled and chopped
1 tablespoon capers, roughly chopped
yolks from 2 hard-boiled eggs

juice of 1/2 lemon
6 tablespoons olive oil
salt and freshly ground black pepper
sufficient cooked pasta to serve 4 people as a starter

---

1 Mince the parsley, basil, celery, onion, capers and egg yolks.

2 Stir in lemon juice and oil to form a thickish sauce.

3 Place in a small saucepan with the seasonings and heat very gently. Spoon over the pasta and serve at once.

PIQUANT SAUCE

Salsa Picante

Cornichons are small French gherkins, but any kind will do.

———— • ————

1 hard-boiled egg, very finely chopped
5–6 anchovy fillets, drained and finely
  chopped
3 tablespoons freshly chopped parsley
3 tablespoons cornichons, very finely
  chopped
2 tablespoons capers, very finely chopped

1 clove garlic, peeled and crushed
juice of ½ lemon
6 tablespoons extra virgin olive oil
¼ teaspoon cayenne pepper
salt and freshly ground black pepper
sufficient cooked pasta to serve 4 people
  as a starter

———— • ————

1 Mix all the chopped ingredients and add the lemon juice, oil, cayenne pepper and seasonings.

2 Place in a small saucepan and heat very gently. Spoon over the pasta and serve at once.

Anchovies

These strongly flavoured little fish can be bought in cans or jars. They may be packed in oil or brine. The latter will need to be soaked in fresh water to remove some of the salt. You can also tone down the flavour of anchovies by soaking them in milk for a while before using them. Discard the soaking liquid.

Most recipes only call for a few anchovies. Those which are packed in oil can be decanted into a dish, topped up with more oil and stored in the fridge. Alternatively you can now buy small jars of Italian anchovy pâté. This has a very soft texture and is ideal for sauces. Use 2–3 tablespoons for a strength of flavour equivalent to a small can of anchovies.

MARINARA SAUCES

Marinara is the Italian word meaning 'of the sea'. It is a useful collective term for the many tuna-based sauces which are so popular in Italy. Like all fish-based sauces they are not usually served with cheese.

TUNA SAUCE

This is the simplest of all the tuna-based sauces. It is popular all over Southern Italy where it is usually served with spaghetti and garnished with a handful of small black olives and a wedge of lemon. Add a basket with chunks of coarse country bread and spoon any extra sauce over these if you are still hungry! Use tuna canned in oil, not brine.

——— • ———

1 × 200g (7oz) can tuna in oil
2 tablespoons extra virgin olive oil
3 tablespoons freshly chopped parsley

150ml (¼ pint) chicken stock
salt and freshly ground black pepper
sufficient cooked pasta to serve 4 people

——— • ———

1 Empty the contents of the can of tuna into a saucepan. Mash with a fork and add the olive oil. Cook gently for 5 minutes.

2 Add the parsley, chicken stock and seasonings and cook for 5 minutes.

3 Spoon over the pasta or toss together and serve at once with more black pepper.

TUNA AND TOMATO SAUCE

This is a more substantial recipe which I picked up near Amalfi. The sauce was the speciality of a little restaurant perched high on the steep hillside overlooking the port. I chose the dish as a main course with a crisp green salad on the side.

——— • ———

1 × 200g (7oz) can tuna in oil
2 tablespoons olive oil
2 onions, peeled and finely chopped
1 clove garlic, peeled and crushed
¼ teaspoon dried oregano
2 teaspoons tomato purée

1 × 225g (8oz) can tomatoes
salt and freshly ground black pepper
2 tablespoons freshly chopped basil
1 tablespoon freshly chopped parsley
sufficient cooked pasta to serve 4 people

1 Drain the oil from the tuna into a pan, add the olive oil and fry the onions and garlic for 4–5 minutes until they turn light gold.

2 Add the oregano, tomato purée and tomatoes. Bring to the boil, season and cook for 15 minutes, stirring occasionally.

3 Flake the tuna into the mixture and cook for a further 5 minutes. Stir in the fresh herbs, spoon over the pasta and serve at once.

Variations

1 Add 3–4 anchovies and fry with the garlic and onions. This gives an even punchier flavour. Omit the basil with this one.

2 Instead of tuna add fresh or canned baby clams to make a Vongole Sauce.

TUNA WITH PRAWNS

This is a richer and slightly more elegant variation on the tuna theme. For the best effect try to keep the tuna in definite flakes. This sauce is good with pasta shells as well as long pasta. Serve with a mixed salad of leaves, shredded peppers and grated carrot.

———— • ————

25g (1oz) butter
125g (4oz) cooked peeled prawns
grated rind of ½ lemon
2 tablespoons freshly chopped parsley
sufficient cooked pasta to serve 4 people

250ml (8fl oz) double cream
salt and freshly ground black pepper
1 × 200g (7oz) can tuna in brine, well drained and carefully flaked

———— • ————

1 Heat the butter in a very large pan and toss the prawns, lemon rind and parsley in the butter for a minute to heat through.

2 Add the pasta, cream and seasonings and toss again over a medium heat.

3 Carefully add the flaked tuna and serve at once.

VONGOLE SAUCE

This seaside classic takes its name from the Italian word *vongola* or clam. Today mussels are usually used as well as clams. Two kinds of clam are found in Italy. One is small with a yellow shell. The other is larger and better flavoured; it is distinguished by a grey shell with a dark blue line through the middle. Both types can usually be found in the UK.

Naples is said to be the homeland of Spaghetti Vongole but my first experience of it was in a tiny harbour-side restaurant in Santa Margharita in the Bay of Genoa. Like this recipe the sauce included tomatoes but some aficionados prefer the sauce 'bianco' or without tomatoes.

———— • ————

1·4kg (3lb) clams or 450g (1lb) clams and 900g (2lb) mussels
salt and freshly ground black pepper
700g (1½lb) ripe tomatoes
2 cloves garlic, peeled and crushed

50g (2fl oz) olive oil
salt and freshly ground black pepper
sufficient cooked pasta to serve 4 people
2 tablespoons freshly chopped parsley

———— • ————

1 Wash the shellfish thoroughly and remove the beards from the mussels if using. If possible leave to stand in cold salted water before using.

2 Place in a large pan and shake over a low heat until all the shells open. Remove from the heat and discard any shells which have not opened. Remove all the shellfish from the pan and take about half of them out of their shells.

3 Blanch, skin and chop the tomatoes.

4 Fry the garlic in the olive oil until lightly browned. Add the tomatoes and seasoning and cook for 10–15 minutes until fairly thick.

5 Add the shellfish (half in their shells and half removed from their shells) and their juices and stir well to coat them with sauce and to heat through.

6 Toss the pasta in this mixture and serve sprinkled with the parsley.

PUTTANESCA SAUCE

This is a gutsy sauce which originated in the slums of Naples. Tradition has it that the recipe was dreamt up by the 'puttanas' or prostitutes who ply their trade in narrow streets around the old port. Its piquant flavour is popular all over Italy and you are as likely to come across it in Milan or Florence as in Naples itself. Despite the relatively long list of ingredients it can be made within 15 minutes. Serve with a side salad of mixed leaves topped with some finely sliced onion rings.

———— • ————

4 tablespoons olive oil
25g (1oz) butter
2 cloves garlic, peeled and crushed
1 small fresh green chilli, seeded and finely chopped
4 anchovy fillets, chopped
450g (1lb) ripe tomatoes, blanched, peeled and diced

1 tablespoon tomato purée
125g (4oz) black olives, stoned and chopped
1 tablespoon capers
sufficient cooked pasta to serve 4 people
2 tablespoons freshly chopped parsley
freshly grated Parmesan cheese

———— • ————

1 Heat the oil and butter in a saucepan and fry the garlic, chilli and anchovies for 2–3 minutes.

2 Add the tomatoes, tomato purée, olives and capers and cook for 6–7 minutes, stirring all the time.

3 Spoon over the pasta. Sprinkle with parsley and serve with freshly grated Parmesan cheese.

Parmesan Cheese

Parmesan is the English name given to Parmigiana Reggiano. It comes from Parma in Emilia Romagna. The cheese is aged for at least a year before it is sold and it hardens and improves in flavour as it matures. Always buy Parmesan in a single piece and grate it just before you need it. Never buy the ready-grated cheese sold in tubs. It tastes like cardboard!

CRAB AND GINGER SAUCE

A really good-quality can of white crabmeat is essential for this exotic starter. The flavours are subtle but delicious. Serve with a delicate side salad of lamb's lettuce dressed with olive oil and a dash of orange juice.

———— • ————

1 × 200g (7oz) can white crabmeat
50g (2oz) butter
a small bunch of spring onions, trimmed
    and chopped
2.5cm (1in) piece fresh root ginger,
    peeled and grated

250ml (8fl oz) double cream
4 tablespoons white wine
salt and freshly ground black pepper
sufficient cooked pasta to serve 4 people
    as a starter

———— • ————

1 Drain the crabmeat and tip onto a plate. Pick over carefully to remove any membrane and bits of shell.

2 Melt the butter in a large saucepan and gently fry the spring onions and root ginger for 2–3 minutes, taking care not to brown them.

3 Pour on the cream and wine and add the seasonings. Bring the mixture to the boil and cook fairly fast for 4–5 minutes to thicken the sauce.

4 Stir in the crabmeat and heat through. Add the pasta and toss well together. Serve with black pepper.

Variation

This dish looks very attractive garnished with small mounds of red lumpfish caviar or, for a special occasion, the juicier keta or salmon caviar now on sale in some supermarkets.

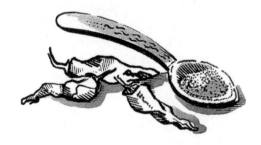

VENETIAN FISH AND FENNEL SAUCE

Whether you are lazing by the Lido in Venice or tramping the hills of Verona you are sure to come across bigoli. It is one of the principal types of local pasta in the Veneto. It is usually served with a simple anchovy and garlic sauce such as that given on page 3 but can also be served with sardines as suggested by Anna del Conte in her book *Scenes from an Italian Kitchen*. The addition of fennel came as I was thinking of ways to use a glut of fennel herb in my father's garden last summer. The result was excellent.

Ask the fishmonger to prepare the fish for you. He may need to descale the fish as well as remove the heads, tails and backbones.

———— • ————

2 cloves garlic, peeled and crushed
4 tablespoons freshly chopped fennel herb or ¼ teaspoon fennel seeds
2 tablespoons freshly chopped parsley
6 tablespoons olive oil
8 large sardines or sprats, filleted by the fishmonger

freshly ground black pepper
sufficient cooked pasta to serve 4 people
juice of 2 lemons
2 tablespoons pine kernels, toasted (see page xi)

———— • ————

1 Fry the garlic and herbs in the oil for a minute. Add the sardines or sprats. Cook for 2 minutes on each side and season with pepper.

2 Toss the pasta in a little more oil and spoon onto 4 plates. Arrange the sardines or sprats on top.

3 Add the lemon juice to the pan. Bring to the boil and pour over the sardines.

4 Garnish with the toasted pine kernels and serve at once.

SOLE WITH CAPERS AND BALSAMIC VINEGAR

Whenever I see small Dover sole in my local fishmonger's I am reminded of the small but tasty Mediterranean sole. Indeed they are the same species but the English seem to prefer their sole much larger and fleshier. Sole is plentiful along the Tuscan coast and this recipe comes from a restaurant alongside the bustling port of Livorno. It is dressed with balsamic vinegar from neighbouring Emilia Romagna. The result is rich and fruity.

Ask the fishmonger to bone, fillet and skin the fish for you but keep the bones to make a fish stock in which to cook the fish.

———— • ————

2 Dover sole, filleted and skinned, with the bones
1 carrot, peeled and sliced
1 onion, peeled and sliced
1 bayleaf
salt and freshly ground black pepper

2 heaped tablespoons capers, drained and washed
sufficient cooked pasta to serve 4 people
6 tablespoons extra virgin olive oil
2 teaspoons balsamic vinegar

———— • ————

1 Break up the fish bones and place in a deep frying pan with the carrot, onion, bayleaf and seasonings. Add about 150ml (¼ pint) water and bring to the boil. Simmer for 10 minutes. Strain and return to the pan.

2 Cut the sole into strips and add to the pan with the fish stock. Poach over a low heat for 2–3 minutes until cooked through.

3 Drain off the liquid, retaining it for a fish soup or sauce another day. Keep the fish warm while you drain the pasta. Then heat the oil very gently in another saucepan.

4 Toss the pasta in half the oil and spoon onto 4 plates. Top with the fish and capers and sprinkle with the rest of the oil and the balsamic vinegar. Serve at once with more black pepper.

MEXICAN PRAWN AND ONION SAUCE

The taste of this Mexican speciality with its lime juice and cayenne pepper is quite different to the traditional flavours of Italy but it still works extremely well with pasta. I usually serve it with spaghettini as an elegant starter. It tastes just as good hot, warm or even cold.

—————— • ——————

2 onions, peeled and thinly sliced
juice and grated rind of 1 lime
1 tablespoon extra virgin olive oil
1 clove garlic, peeled and crushed
2 tablespoons white wine vinegar
a pinch of dried oregano

salt and freshly ground black pepper
a pinch of cayenne or hot paprika
20 large peeled prawns
sufficient pasta to serve 4 people as a
   starter

—————— • ——————

1 Steep the onions and grated lime rind in the lime juice for as long as you have time.

2 Pour the liquid off the onions and set aside.

3 Heat the oil in a frying pan and fry the garlic for 1 minute. Remove from the heat and add the onions. Stir and return to the heat. Cook for 2 minutes, stirring all the time.

4 Add all the remaining ingredients except the prawns, pasta and juices from the onion. Bring to the boil; add the prawns and onion juice and toss well together.

5 Spoon over the pasta. Add more oil and toss well. Serve with more black pepper on the side.

ITALIAN MEAT SAUCE

Italy has many meat-based sauces for pasta, but Bolognaise is the most famous. It is also the only one to have been officially standardised. The official recipe, kept at the Chamber of Commerce in Bologna, requires lean minced veal with onion; celery, carrot and prosciutto fried in butter; tomatoes; lemon zest and nutmeg. A dash of cream is added at the end to bind the mixture.

All Italian cooks have their own versions of the recipe but they all agree that the original was cooked in an earthenware pot for as long as possible. However Elizabeth David, in her book *Italian Food*, manages to come up with an authentic recipe which only takes 30 minutes to cook. Here is my version. It, too, can be cooked in 30 minutes, but if you do have longer to spare it will improve with extra cooking; add more stock if it shows signs of drying up.

CLASSIC BOLOGNAISE SAUCE

In Bologna this sauce is mainly used in lasagne but in the rest of Italy, and indeed the world, it has come to be used mainly with spaghetti. This version freezes well so make a double quantity and simply thaw and reheat for a really quick meal.

Unsmoked pancetta or unsmoked bacon can be used in place of prosciutto crudo. If so, fry in the butter first, before adding the vegetables.

———————— • ————————

25g (1oz) butter
1 onion, peeled and finely chopped
1 small carrot, peeled and finely chopped
2 sticks of celery, trimmed and finely chopped
75g (3oz) prosciutto crudo, diced
450g (1lb) lean minced beef
150ml (¼ pint) red wine

1½ tablespoons tomato purée, mixed with 50ml (2fl oz) water
¼ teaspoon grated lemon rind
a pinch of grated nutmeg
salt and freshly ground black pepper
2 tablespoons double cream
sufficient cooked pasta to serve 4 people
freshly grated Parmesan cheese

———————— • ————————

1 Melt the butter in a pan and gently fry the onion, carrot and celery for 3–4 minutes. Add the prosciutto and cook for another minute or so.

2 Next add the meat and seal all over, before adding all the remaining sauce ingredients except the cream. Bring to the boil, reduce the heat and simmer, uncovered, for 30 minutes.

3 Stir in the cream and toss the pasta in the sauce. Top with a knob of butter and serve with grated Parmesan.

EVERYDAY MEAT SAUCE

If you do not have all the ingredients to hand for the recipe given above and your local Italian deli is not really local, here is a simple but still very tasty meat sauce for spaghetti.

———— • ————

2 rashers unsmoked bacon (optional), diced
2 tablespoons olive oil
2 cloves garlic, peeled and finely chopped
1 onion, peeled and finely chopped
450g (1lb) lean minced beef
2 tablespoons tomato purée

¼ teaspoon dried oregano or wild marjoram
salt and freshly ground black pepper
a pinch of grated nutmeg (optional)
1 × 400g (14oz) can tomatoes
4 tablespoons red wine or beef stock
sufficient cooked pasta to serve 4 people

———— • ————

1 Fry the diced bacon, if using, in the oil and add the garlic and onion. Brown lightly.

2 Add the meat and cook for 3–4 minutes until well sealed.

3 Add all the remaining sauce ingredients and bring to the boil. Simmer with the lid off for 20 minutes. Stir from time to time.

4 Toss the pasta in the sauce and serve.

Variation

Add 125g (4oz) button mushrooms, finely chopped, with the tomatoes.

CHICKEN LIVERS WITH LEEKS AND RED WINE

This dish was one of the specialities of the luncheon menu of the Orangery Restaurant at the Christopher Wren Hotel in Windsor. Instead of oil or cream the sauce is based on a well-flavoured meat stock. Char-grilled peppers and chicken livers are not tossed with the pasta but arranged in an attractive pattern on top. The result is unusual but very appetising, and works best with spaghettini. Despite its apparent complexity the dish can still be produced in just under half an hour. Serve with a bowl of lightly cooked warm spinach leaves tossed in lemon juice.

———— • ————

2 red peppers, quartered and seeded
2 large leeks, trimmed and cut into 6cm (2¹/₂in) lengths
2 tablespoons olive oil
salt and freshly ground black pepper

12 chicken livers
150ml (¹/₄ pint) strong beef stock
3 tablespoons red wine
sufficient cooked pasta to serve 4 people
a few sprigs of fresh chervil

———— • ————

1 Place the peppers skin side up under a hot grill and leave until quite well charred. Pile into a bowl and leave for 10–15 minutes. Remove all the skin and cut into long thin strips. Keep warm.

2 Steam the leeks in a little boiling, salted water or in a steamer basket until they are almost cooked. Cut into long thin strips and keep warm.

3 Heat the oil in a pan and gently fry the seasoned chicken livers, turning occasionally. When they are cooked but still pinkish in the middle, remove from the pan and keep warm.

4 Pour the stock and wine into the pan and bring to the boil, stirring all the time. Boil the mixture for 3–4 minutes to reduce. Taste and correct the seasoning.

5 Pile the pasta onto the centre of 4 plates. Cut the chicken livers in half and arrange round the edge of each plate.

6 Sprinkle the lengths of leek over the top and arrange the grilled pepper strips in the centre.

7 Pour the juices from the saucepan over each plate and dot with sprigs of chervil. Serve at once.

·CHAPTER THREE·

LONG FLAT PASTA

ong flat pasta varies from wide noodles with fluted edges, through the popular tagliatelle, to the much finer linguine. It is often, but not always, made with egg and may be flavoured with spinach to produce green pasta or tomato to give pale pink pasta.

This type of pasta is traditionally served with thicker sauces based on cream, cheese or eggs. The Italians also serve tagliatelle with meat-based sauces.

All the types of pasta listed below are available dried and some of them are sold fresh. Not many are made with wholemeal flour.

For cooking instructions, see page xi.

TAGLIATELLE

This is the classic egg noodle of Emilia Romagna. It has travelled the world in various forms. For centuries the exact width of tagliatelle was argued over, but in 1972 a gastronomic law was passed in Italy whereby a strand of tagliatelle has to measure 8mm across when cooked. This means that it must be no more than 6.5–7mm when uncooked to allow it to swell during cooking. Any pasta not conforming to these measurements must be sold under another name.

Tagliatelle may be packed in straight medium-sized lengths or in curled bundles or nests and it may be plain or flavoured. Like spaghetti it is extremely versatile and can be used with most of the quick sauces in Chapter 1.

NOODLES

This is the general term often given to tagliatelle-like pasta which does not conform to the correct measurements.

PAPPARDELLE

This is a very wide tagliatelle which is often served in Tuscany. It is usually home-made but can occasionally be bought ready-made.

FETTUCINE

This is the Roman version of tagliatelle. It is traditionally made a little narrower and a little thicker. In the Veneto this type of pasta is called *paparele*.

LINGUINE

Linguine is also known as *bavette* in Tuscany. It is much thinner than tagliatelle, being only about 3mm (⅛in) wide. It needs a more delicate sauce or it will be swamped. It is also used in soups and soufflés. *Tagliolini* is a home-made version.

TRENETTE

Falling somewhere between tagliatelle and linguine, this Ligurian speciality is *the* pasta to partner Pesto Sauce (see pages 52–3). However elsewhere it can be used with any of the quick sauces given in Chapter 1. Not content with adding plenty of herbs to their sauces, the Ligurians also add fresh herbs to trenette dough to make the speckled *trenette verde*.

LASAGNETTE

Popular in Southern Italy in Calabria, this long dried pasta is about 2cm (¾in) wide, with attractively fluted edges. It is served with fairly robust, often meat-based, sauces.

FRESH CHEESE AND TOMATO SAUCE

The fresh flavours of this virtually uncooked sauce are quite delicious in the summer sunshine. Serve as a starter with linguine or double up to make a substantial main course with a salad of sliced peppers, black olives and cucumber.

———————— • ————————

4–5 tablespoons extra virgin olive oil
4 spring onions, trimmed and finely chopped
225g (8oz) ricotta cheese, diced
4 medium-sized fresh ripe tomatoes, diced

leaves from 6 large sprigs of basil, roughly torn
salt and freshly ground black pepper
sufficient cooked pasta to serve 4 people as a starter

———————— • ————————

1 Gently heat the oil in a pan and add the spring onions and ricotta. After about 1 minute stir in the tomatoes, basil and seasonings.

2 Remove from the heat as soon as the mixture begins to warm through. Toss with the pasta, and serve at once.

Variation

Use a fresh goat's cheese in place of ricotta cheese.

Ricotta Cheese

Ricotta is known as cheese but is in fact a by product of cheese-making. It is made from the whey which is left after the curds have been made into cheese. Cow's milk ricotta is very crumbly; ewe's milk ricotta is much creamier. Both have a very delicate fresh flavour. Delicatessens and many supermarkets stock them.

EAST-WEST SAUCE

This Californian recipe mixes the flavours of East and West with excellent results and is best served with trenette. The original used rice vinegar but this can sometimes be difficult to find. Finish the meal with a mixture of tropical fruit.

———— • ————

5 tablespoons peanut oil
1 tablespoon Oriental roasted sesame oil
1 whole dried red chilli
225g (8oz) broccoli, cut into florets
125g (4oz) mangetout
1 large red pepper, seeded and diced

3 tablespoons soy sauce
3 tablespoons rice vinegar or white wine
  vinegar
sufficient cooked pasta to serve 4 people
3 eggs, beaten
a few sprigs of fresh coriander

———— • ————

1 Heat the oils in a large pan. Fry the chilli for 1 minute, then remove from the pan and discard.

2 Toss the vegetables into the oil and stir-fry for 2–3 minutes.

3 Pour on the soy sauce and vinegar and bring to the boil. Add the pasta and toss together. Add the eggs and toss again.

4 Serve garnished with the sprigs of fresh coriander.

Variations

1 Add a few drops of Tabasco Sauce for a hotter result.

2 Add the grated rind and juice of 1 orange with the soy sauce and vinegar.

TUSCAN BROAD BEAN SAUCE

Broad beans are a great favourite in Tuscany where this sauce would be served with wide noodles or pappardelle. They crop up in soups, stews and sauces like this one. They are even served raw as an accompaniment to the local Pecorino cheese. In Tuscany only fresh beans in season are used; small frozen beans can be substituted, but you will need to remove their skins.

———————— • ————————

350g (12oz) fresh or frozen broad beans
3–4 shallots or 1 small onion, peeled and very finely chopped
1 stick celery, trimmed and very finely chopped
25g (1oz) butter

150ml (¼ pint) double cream
50ml (2fl oz) strong vegetable or chicken stock
salt and freshly ground black pepper
3 tablespoons freshly chopped parsley
sufficient cooked pasta to serve 4 people

———————— • ————————

1 Cover the broad beans with water and bring to the boil. Drain and, if necessary, slip off the skins.

2 Fry the shallots or onion and celery in the butter for 3–4 minutes to soften.

3 Add the prepared broad beans, cream and stock and bring to the boil. Simmer for 5 minutes. Stir in the seasoning and parsley and pour over the pasta. Serve at once.

Variations

1 For a less rich but still very pleasing sauce, substitute olive oil for butter and omit the cream. Increase the quantity of stock to 150ml (¼ pint) and add 1 teaspoon cornflour.

2 In winter the Tuscans add a handful of wild mushrooms to this recipe. Put in at the last minute.

FRESH BEANS AND TOMATO SAUCE

Tiny young French beans are mixed with fresh broad beans to give an attractive appearance to this simple tagliatelle sauce from San Gimignano in the heart of Tuscany. You can see at least two of the seven distinctive towers of this famous walled hill town from the restaurants in the main square. The towers were built by successful citizens to show off their wealth.

I had this dish as a starter in one of those restaurants. We followed it with spatchcock poussins grilled with fresh sage and flambéed with a little grappa. A bottle of the local Vernaccia di San Gimignano completed the meal.

———————— • ————————

175g (6oz) fresh or frozen broad beans
175g (6oz) fresh green or French beans,
topped and tailed and cut into long
thin strips
½ quantity Tuscan Tomato and Basil
Sauce (see page 23)

3 tablespoons double cream (optional)
sufficient cooked pasta to serve 4 people
freshly grated Parmesan cheese
freshly ground black pepper

———————— • ————————

1 Blanch the broad beans in boiling water for 3 minutes and slip off the skins if necessary.

2 Return to the pan with the green beans and cook for a further 5–6 minutes until just tender.

3 Heat the Tomato Sauce in a large saucepan. Add the cream if using and the drained beans. Heat through again.

4 Add the pasta and toss well together. Serve with grated Parmesan and black pepper.

SAUTÉED MUSHROOMS WITH BALSAMIC VINEGAR

I first had this simple dish in a restaurant in the Piazza Fiore not far from the Tiber in Rome. Large piles of fresh porcini or wild mushrooms decorated a side table and I realised for the first time how large these mushrooms can be. They were at least 15cm (6in) across, and some were larger. The dish can also be made with cremini, which are similar but less flavoursome.

Both these types of mushrooms are expensive and difficult to get in the UK so I have worked out a mixture of large cultivated mushrooms for texture and mixed dried wild mushrooms for flavour. Serve with wide, flat noodles and a green salad.

———— • ————

25g (1oz) dried mixed wild mushrooms
1 clove garlic, peeled and crushed
4 tablespoons freshly chopped parsley
4 tablespoons olive oil
225g (8 oz) large fleshy cup mushrooms,
* halved and sliced*

½ teaspoon balsamic vinegar
salt and freshly ground black pepper
sufficient pasta to serve 4 people as a
* starter*

———— • ————

1 Barely cover the wild mushrooms with boiling water and leave to stand for 15–20 minutes. Drain, retaining the liquid.

2 Gently fry the garlic and parsley in the olive oil, and after 1–2 minutes add both types of mushrooms. Continue to cook over a medium heat, stirring fairly frequently.

3 Mix the balsamic vinegar with the mushroom juices and add to the pan. Season and toss over a high heat for 1–2 minutes. Spoon over the cooked pasta.

Balsamic Vinegar

Real balsamic vinegar is made in private estates in Emilia Romagna and is both very difficult to find and very expensive. It is made from unfermented grape juice and is aged in a series of wooden casks for at least 12 years. Commercial balsamic vinegar is made in a number of factories. It is not aged for anything like as long as the traditional vinegar. Some brands are quite good but others are very bad. A reasonably good version will cost £8–£10 for a smallish bottle but the good news is that it has such an intense fruity flavour that you really do not need to use very much.

PESTO SAUCES

This Ligurian speciality is on the menu of every coastal restaurant from San Remo to Genoa. Each one offers its own variation on the classic sauce but what is essential is a large quantity of fresh basil. If you do not have a garden you will need two or even three potted plants!

In Liguria there are those who say you should only make this sauce when the basil is in flower but that would mean losing an excellent sauce for the rest of the year. Pesto sauce can be served with almost any kind of long flat pasta, though trenette, the Ligurian tagliatelle, probably just about wins on points. Traditionally, sliced potatoes were cooked with the pasta and then both were drained and tossed in the Pesto Sauce.

All three of the following sauces will keep for a week or more in the fridge.

CLASSIC PESTO SAUCE

Here's the most famous version.

———— • ————

45–50 basil leaves (8–10 large sprigs)
1/4 teaspoon salt
1–2 cloves garlic to taste, peeled
25g (1oz) pine kernels

15g (1/2oz) freshly grated Parmesan cheese
50ml (2fl oz) extra virgin olive oil
freshly ground black pepper
sufficient cooked pasta to serve 4 people

———— • ————

1 Put all the sauce ingredients into a blender or food processor and blend until you have a smooth green purée.

2 If the sauce is too thick add a little more oil.

3 Toss the pasta in the sauce over a low heat and serve.

Variations

1 Substitute Pecorino Sardo for half the Parmesan to give a more pungent flavour.

2 Stone and quarter 20 black olives, and toss with the sauce and pasta.

TUSCAN PESTO

In Tuscany pine kernels are often replaced by walnuts to produce the region's own version of Pesto Sauce. It is usually served with spaghetti. Make sure you buy really fresh walnuts for this dish. Any incipient rancid flavours will be magnified once the sauce hits the hot pasta.

———— • ————

45–50 basil leaves (8–10 large sprigs)
75g (3oz) shelled walnuts
15g (¹/₂oz) freshly grated Parmesan cheese

75ml (3fl oz) extra virgin olive oil
salt and freshly ground black pepper
sufficient cooked pasta to serve 4 people

———— • ————

1 Place all the sauce ingredients in a blender or food processor and blend for 1–2 minutes.

2 Add more oil if the sauce is too thick.

3 Toss the pasta in the sauce over a low heat and serve.

AMERICAN CILANTRO SAUCE

Cilantro is the American name for fresh coriander leaves and these are used to make a really pungent Californian pesto sauce. You do not need to use too much of it!

———— • ————

a bunch of fresh coriander (approx. 40g (1¹/₂oz))
2 cloves garlic, peeled
25g (1oz) pine kernels

25g (1oz) freshly grated Parmesan cheese
50ml (2fl oz) extra virgin olive oil
salt and freshly ground black pepper
sufficient cooked pasta to serve 4 people

———— • ————

1 Wash the coriander and dry on kitchen paper. Use the stalks as well as the leaves.

2 Place all the sauce ingredients in a blender or food processor and blend for 1–2 minutes.

3 Add more oil if the sauce is too thick.

4 Toss the pasta in the sauce over a low heat and serve.

MUSHROOMS WITH WHISKY

The inspiration for this dish comes from Scotland rather than Italy. It is the creation of an Edinburgh chef who has a passion for both wild mushrooms and his native brew and decided to put the two together. The rich and pungent sauce makes a great starter. It goes well with both linguine and spaghettini.

———— • ————

25g (1oz) dried mixed wild mushrooms
1 tablespoon whisky
15g (½ oz) butter
1 clove garlic, peeled and crushed
1 tablespoon freshly chopped parsley

4 tablespoons double cream
sufficient cooked pasta to serve 4 people
as a starter
freshly ground black pepper

———— • ————

1 Pour 4 tablespoons boiling water over the mushrooms to just cover them. Leave to stand for 20 minutes. Add the whisky and allow to steep for another 30 minutes.

2 Melt the butter in a pan and lightly fry the garlic and parsley. Add the mushrooms and their juices to the pan.

3 Stir in the double cream and bring to the boil. Continue cooking on a fairly high heat until the sauce has thickened.

4 Mix thoroughly with the pasta and serve with plenty of freshly ground black pepper.

Porcini

Porcini are one of the popular wild mushrooms of Italy. They are very large and fleshy and have a distinctive earthy flavour. They are usually pretty expensive even in their dried form. Packets of mixed wild mushrooms are on sale in plenty of specialist grocers and delicatessen shops and they tend to be rather cheaper.

PUMPKIN SAUCE

The pumpkins which are widely grown in Lombardy usually have green skin and bright yellow flesh, though there is a variety grown in Southern Italy which is pale green throughout. They are used in soups, pasta dishes and risottos. The orange-skinned variety available in other countries works just as well. Remember to weigh the pumpkin flesh after you have removed the thick skin and the seeds. An 800g (1¾lb) pumpkin will give about 450g (1lb) flesh.

A side dish of steamed broccoli florets tossed in olive oil gives a good contrast of colours and textures. Parmesan is not served with this sauce.

———— • ————

3 cloves garlic, peeled and crushed
1 onion, peeled and finely chopped
1 tablespoon olive oil
450g (1lb) pumpkin flesh, peeled, seeded
 and diced
250ml (8fl oz) strong vegetable stock

2 tablespoons freshly chopped parsley
100ml (4fl oz) single cream
¼ teaspoon grated nutmeg
salt and freshly ground black pepper
sufficient cooked pasta to serve 4 people

———— • ————

1 Gently fry the garlic and onion in the oil for 3–4 minutes to soften. Do not allow them to burn.

2 Add the pumpkin and vegetable stock and bring to the boil. Cover and simmer over a medium heat for 15 minutes, stirring occasionally, until the pumpkin is tender.

3 Break up by beating with a wooden spoon and stir in the parsley, cream, nutmeg and seasoning. Cook for a further minute and add a little of the pasta cooking water if the sauce is too thick. Pour over the pasta. Toss well together and serve at once.

Variation

Use whole garlic cloves and gently fry with a roughly chopped, seeded red chilli pepper for 2–3 minutes. Remove the garlic and chilli from the oil and continue as above. If you like a really hot sauce include the seeds of the chilli pepper.

ROMAN SAUCE

I first had this rather unusual pasta topping in a pretty restaurant nestling under the garden walls of the Villa d'Este in Rome. Swiss chard is eaten quite often in this city. Spinach could also be used but it tends to go soggy too quickly and its stalks do not give the same texture to the dish. This sauce is best served as a first course with fettucine.

———— • ————

350g (12oz) Swiss chard, washed
4 tablespoons olive oil
1 clove garlic, peeled and chopped
2 tablespoons pine kernels

2 tablespoons raisins
salt and freshly ground black pepper
sufficient cooked pasta to serve 4 people
  as a starter

———— • ————

1 Cut the stalks from the chard and slice fairly thinly. Set aside.

2 Cook the leaves in a dry saucepan for 3–4 minutes until just cooked. Squeeze dry and chop very roughly.

3 Heat the oil in a frying pan and fry the garlic for 1 minute. Add the pine kernels and continue frying until they begin to brown.

4 Toss the sliced chard stalks into the pan and continue frying for 2–3 minutes until they soften. Add the chard leaves, raisins and seasoning, and toss over a medium heat for a further 2 minutes.

5 Spoon onto the pasta and serve at once with more black pepper.

Variation

Use a little less oil and dress with 2–3 tablespoons double cream just before serving.

FRESH SORREL AND FETA CHEESE SAUCE

I am lucky that sorrel grows well in my father's garden but it really is worth searching out some fresh sorrel for this deliciously tangy recipe. Some supermarkets sell it during the summer months. Otherwise raid a friend's garden!

This sauce can be served with any kind of noodle but it goes particularly well with broad flat noodles or lasagnette. Start the meal with some grilled vegetables or a plate of Parma ham and melon.

———— • ————

1 large onion, peeled and very finely sliced
2 tablespoons olive oil
8–10 large leaves fresh sorrel, shredded
300g (10oz) Feta cheese, crumbled

6 tablespoons vegetable stock
freshly ground black pepper
sufficient cooked pasta to serve 4 people

———— • ————

1 Gently fry the onion in the oil until soft but not brown.

2 Stir in the sorrel, Feta, stock and pepper and bring to the boil. Continue stirring until the cheese has half melted into the stock. The consistency should be creamy but lumpy!

3 Toss together with the pasta and serve at once.

Vegetable Stock

There are a few vegetable stock cubes on sale which are not too full of salt or monosodium glutamate but home-made stock is better. I keep all the cooking water from my vegetables and then, from time to time, boil it up with well-fried vegetables such as carrot, onion and celery and any greens or herbs which are getting past their best. Strain, taste, and boil again if the flavour is not strong enough. A useful way to freeze stock is to pour it into ice cube trays. You will then easily be able to use large or small quantities depending on the recipe.

PEASANT'S SAUCE

Every region of Italy has its own Paesana or Peasant's Sauce. They are all vegetable-based and very quick and easy to make. I just use any vegetables I have to hand so that some days it resembles the recipe exactly and other days it almost seems like another dish.

It's fun to use a mixture of egg, spinach and tomato noodles or tagliatelle with this sauce. The rainbow effect is very attractive.

——— • ———

2 tablespoons cooking oil
1 onion, peeled and sliced
1 red pepper, seeded and thinly sliced
1 green pepper, seeded and thinly sliced

salt and freshly ground black pepper
sufficient cooked pasta to serve 4 people
2 eggs, beaten
freshly grated Parmesan cheese

——— • ———

1 Heat the oil and fry the onion for 2 minutes until soft but not brown.

2 Add the peppers, and any of the optional extras you wish (see below), and continue to fry gently for 5–6 minutes, stirring from time to time until the vegetables have softened.

3 Season, add the pasta and the eggs and toss well over the heat. Serve at once with plenty of black pepper and Parmesan.

Optional Extras

3 tablespoons frozen peas
3 tablespoons frozen sweetcorn
125g (4oz) button mushrooms, sliced or
   quartered

2–3 tomatoes, coarsely chopped
75g (3oz) chopped ham

CHINESE SAUCE

You can use Chinese egg noodles or Italian egg noodles with this Chinese-style stir-fried topping. If you are not used to using tofu you could use Greek Haloumi cheese instead but add it at the very last minute or it will go too hard. Start the meal with spring rolls or prawn toasts.

———— • ————

3 tablespoons peanut oil
2 teaspoons freshly grated root ginger
2 cloves garlic, peeled and crushed
1 bunch spring onions, trimmed and sliced lengthways
1 tablespoon cornflour
salt and freshly ground black pepper
225g (8oz) block tofu, cut into cubes
75g (3oz) mangetout
1 green pepper, seeded and cut into strips

4 leaves Chinese cabbage
8 leaves Swiss chard, shredded
2 tablespoons cashew nuts, toasted (see page xi)
2 tablespoons light soy sauce
4 tablespoons well-flavoured vegetable stock
sufficient cooked pasta to serve 4 people
a few sprigs of fresh parsley and chervil

———— • ————

1 Heat the oil in a large wok or frying pan and stir-fry the ginger, garlic and spring onion for 1 minute.

2 Mix the cornflour and seasoning and carefully toss the tofu cubes in this.

3 Add to the frying pan and fry on all sides.

4 Add all the vegetables, nuts, soy sauce and stock and bring to the boil. Boil fast for 1–2 minutes. Spoon over the pasta and serve garnished with the sprigs of parsley and chervil.

TUNA AND WHITE BEAN SAUCE

The inspiration for this filling sauce comes from a salad I had in Southern Spain. I liked the combination of flavours so much that I wanted to serve it as a hot dish as well as a cold salad. Here is the hot version I came up with to serve with wide noodles. Accompany with a simple mixed salad.

———— • ————

4 tablespoons olive oil
1 clove garlic, peeled and crushed
2 shallots or 4–5 spring onions, trimmed and finely chopped
1 bayleaf
175g (6oz) courgettes, diced
1 × 400g (14oz) can tuna in brine, drained and flaked

1 × 400g (14oz) can white kidney beans or cannellini beans, well drained
1 tablespoon capers
salt and freshly ground black pepper
sufficient cooked pasta to serve 4 people
3 tablespoons freshly chopped parsley

———— • ————

1 Heat the oil in a pan and gently fry the garlic, shallots or spring onions and the bayleaf for 3–4 minutes. Do not allow the vegetables to brown. Remove the bayleaf.

2 Add the diced courgettes and toss over a low heat for a further 3–4 minutes.

3 Next stir in all the remaining ingredients, except the pasta and parsley, and heat carefully over a medium heat. Turn with a fork but take care not to break up the tuna too much or mash the beans.

4 Serve spooned over the pasta with more olive oil on the side. Top with the fresh parsley.

SALMON WITH NUTMEG AND DILL

This special occasion dish comes from the Silver Plate Restaurant in New York where it is a firm favourite with the customers. It is very quick to make and is great for entertaining. Serve with tagliatelle. Add a side dish of sliced cucumber, or steamed fennel sprinkled with a little lemon juice, for a memorable meal.

————— • —————

300ml (½ pint) double cream
50g (2oz) butter
4 tablespoons white wine
salt and freshly ground black pepper
a pinch of grated nutmeg

2 tablespoons freshly grated Parmesan
cheese
4 tablespoons freshly chopped dill
350g (12oz) freshly cooked salmon,
flaked
sufficient cooked pasta to serve 4 people
a few sprigs of fresh dill

————— • —————

1 Pour the cream into a saucepan and add the butter, wine, seasonings and nutmeg. Bring to the boil and cook until it is reduced by about a third.

2 Stir in the cheese and chopped dill and then very carefully fold in the salmon.

3 Arrange the pasta on 4 plates and top with the salmon cream sauce. Decorate with the sprigs of fresh dill.

Variations

1 Use 3 tablespoons sweet Martini or Cinzano Bianco in place of wine.

2 Use fresh tarragon instead of dill.

SOLE IN TOMATO SAUCE

This is a well-flavoured sauce which comes from Brindisi on the Adriatic coast of Italy. The basic tomato sauce is packed with anchovies, olives and extra garlic. It is usually made with sole or monkfish. I chose lemon sole for everyday use as it is much more economical than Mediterranean or Dover sole.

———— • ————

4 tablespoons olive oil
1–2 cloves garlic, peeled and crushed
4 anchovy fillets, drained and chopped
½ quantity Simple Tomato Sauce from
  Naples (see page 22)

12 black olives, stoned and halved
freshly ground black pepper
2 lemon sole, filleted and skinned
sufficient cooked pasta to serve 4 people
4 heaped teaspoons soured cream

———— • ————

1 Heat the oil in a deep frying pan and add the garlic and anchovies. Fry for 1–2 minutes, stirring all the time. Add the Tomato Sauce, olives and pepper and bring to the boil.

2 Cut each fillet into 3–4 pieces and carefully place in the sauce. Cover and simmer for 4–5 minutes until the fish is cooked through.

3 Arrange the pasta on 4 plates and spoon the pieces of fish and the sauce over the top. Top each plate with a teaspoonful of soured cream and serve at once.

TUSCAN CHICKPEA SAUCE

Chickpeas are popular in many parts of Italy and they turn up rather surprisingly in as many pasta dishes as soups or side dishes. Because they are quite chunky they go well with pasta shapes (see pages 91 and 92). However this sauce from Tuscany uses a mixture of puréed and whole chickpeas to make an unusual sauce for long flat noodles, the broader the better. You can easily rustle this up in the time it takes to cook the pasta and still have time to prepare a simple green salad.

———— • ————

1 × 400g (14oz) can chickpeas, drained
3 tablespoons olive oil
1 clove garlic, peeled and cut in half
2 large sprigs of fresh rosemary
4 rashers smoked pancetta or streaky bacon, diced

1 large onion, peeled and finely chopped
3 tablespoons double cream
2 tablespoons dry white wine
salt and freshly ground black pepper
sufficient cooked pasta to serve 4 people
freshly grated Pecorino Romano cheese

———— • ————

1 Purée half the chickpeas in a blender or food processor and roughly chop the rest.

2 Heat the oil in a large saucepan and fry the garlic and rosemary over a gentle heat for 1–2 minutes. Remove with a slotted spoon. Add the pancetta or bacon and fry until crisp. Add the onion and continue frying for 3–4 minutes.

3 Stir in the cream and wine and both the puréed and chopped chickpeas. Season to taste.

4 Toss the pasta in the mixture and serve at once with plenty of grated Pecorino.

CARBONARA SAUCE

There are all kinds of stories about the origins of this Roman speciality. One version credits Umbrian charcoal burners (the carbonari) with its invention: all the ingredients are easy to carry around and they could have cooked it over their open fires.

Another version suggests that the dish was invented during the war, in response to the American allies' demands for 'ham and eggs'. Whatever the truth of this story, the soldiers liked the dish so much that they took the recipe back home with them.

Recipes vary but the 'ham' is usually pancetta or unsmoked streaky bacon. However I have seen recipes which use coppa (cured shoulder of pork), prosciutto and even cooked ham. I am very fond of serving this sauce with fettucine but the classic choice would probably be spaghetti. Other cooks team it up with macaroni, penne or rigatoni. There should be sufficient heat in the pasta to cook the eggs to the right consistency. They can even be added after the pasta has been taken off the hob.

———— • ————

125g (4oz) pancetta or unsmoked streaky bacon, diced
1 tablespoon olive oil or melted butter
2 size 1 eggs, beaten

25g (1oz) freshly grated Parmesan cheese
salt and freshly ground black pepper
sufficient cooked pasta to serve 4 people as a starter

———— • ————

1 Cook the bacon in the oil or butter until crisp. Mix the eggs, cheese and seasoning.

2 Drain the pasta and toss with the hot bacon and its fat. Stir in the egg and cheese mixture. Toss well.

3 Serve at once with more Parmesan and black pepper.

Variation

Add a little chopped onion when you fry the bacon or, if you are vegetarian, use instead of the bacon.

GRASS AND HAY

The name of this modern pasta dish actually refers to the mixture of fresh green and yellow egg noodles rather than the sauce. They are often served simply with butter or cream. However if you have a little time try this version from Sienna; it will not take you more than half an hour and it makes a good dinner party dish.

———— • ————

125g (4oz) unsmoked bacon, diced
125g (4oz) prosciutto, diced
2 tablespoons olive oil
1 onion, peeled and finely chopped
1 carrot, peeled and finely chopped
1 stalk celery, trimmed and finely chopped

125g (4oz) brown mushrooms, finely chopped
1 × 400g (14oz) can tomatoes
150ml (¼ pint) white wine
125g (4oz) frozen peas
freshly ground black pepper
sufficient cooked pasta to serve 4 people

———— • ————

1 Dry fry the bacon in a deep saucepan until crisp. Add the prosciutto and then the oil.

2 Next add the onion, carrot and celery and continue frying gently for 5 minutes, stirring from time to time. Add the mushrooms and fry for a further 2 minutes.

3 Add the tomatoes and white wine and bring to the boil. Simmer fast, uncovered, for 15 minutes.

4 Add the peas and black pepper and simmer for another 1–2 minutes. Pour over the pasta and serve.

TUBULAR PASTA

There are both long and short varieties of tubular or hollow pasta. However the longer types are always broken into shorter lengths before cooking. This allows the sauce to work its way inside the smaller pieces.

Good sauces for this type of pasta usually have plenty of juice to run into the centre of the tubes. Medium-sized tubular pasta is often served with vegetable-based sauces but the larger penne and rigatoni will take rich meat and fish sauces.

All the types of pasta listed below are available dried but they can only rarely be bought fresh. There are also wholemeal versions of some of them.

For cooking instructions, see page xi.

MACARONI

This is probably the best known tubular pasta outside Italy. For the Italian market it is sold in lengths of about 23–25cm (9–10in) but it is intended to be broken into 10cm (4in) pieces. Outside Italy, macaroni of varying thicknesses is usually sold ready cut into short straight or curved pieces. The latter is known as elbow macaroni.

ZITI

This is really the Southern Italian name for a fairly delicate macaroni. It comes in 23–25cm (9–10in) lengths and is very popular in Sicily.

BUCATINI

This is a long thick pasta with hollow strands which is popular in Central and Southern Italy. In the latter it is known as *perciatelli*. Like ziti it should be broken into smaller lengths before use.

PENNE

This short tubular pasta has a smooth surface and the pieces are cut at an angle to look like quills. They are usually served with thick or rich sauces which will penetrate the hollows. *Pennete* is a shorter thinner version.

RIGATONI

These 5–8cm (2–3in) tubes are ridged along their length in order to catch some of the sauce. *Marille* is a double rigatoni created by an Italian car designer. *Ditali* are short rigatoni about 1cm (½in) long.

GARGANELLI

This is a home-made pasta from Emilia Romagna. The rolled pasta dough is cut into squares, curled round a stick and then combed to produce a ridged effect. *Trofie* is a similar pasta made in Liguria and other areas.

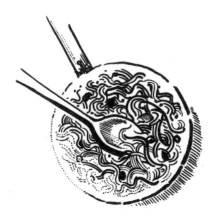

CAULIFLOWER AND GRILLED RED PEPPER

The idea for this sauce came from a salad served at Orso, one of the new wave Italian-style restaurants in Covent Garden. I like the punchy combination of olives, red peppers and cauliflower even better with pasta and it looks particularly attractive with elbow macaroni. Use the discarded cauliflower stalks to make soup.

———— • ————

2 large red peppers, seeded and quartered
1 large cauliflower, cut into florets
20 black olives
6 tablespoons double cream

4 sprigs fresh tarragon, chopped
sufficient cooked pasta to serve 4 people
4 large sprigs fresh broadleaf parsley

———— • ————

1 Grill the peppers until the skin chars. Leave to stand and then peel off the skin. Cut into strips.

2 Cook the cauliflower for 1–1½ minutes in boiling salted water. It should still have some bite to it.

3 Stone the olives and cut into quarters.

4 Place the cauliflower florets, pepper strips and olives in a saucepan and add the double cream. Bring to the boil and add the tarragon.

5 Spoon over your chosen pasta and decorate each plate with a sprig of broadleaf parsley.

Olives

Olives are grown in almost every province of Italy. The green ones are picked before they are fully ripe; all olives darken as they mature. Olives are hard and bitter when they are picked but table olives are cured for many months in huge vats of salt and water. The flavour of green and black olives can be quite different and they are not really interchangeable in recipes.

COURGETTE AND RED ONION SAUCE

You can vary the flavour of this simple vegetable sauce by using different herbs. I have tried fresh dill, tarragon and mint with quite different results. Whichever you choose you will need to use quite a lot of it. Serve after a platter of prosciutto. My favourite pasta with this sauce is ziti.

———— • ————

2 red onions, peeled and sliced
4 tablespoons olive oil
225g (8oz) courgettes, trimmed and cut
* into matchsticks*

a handful of fresh herbs, chopped
salt and freshly ground black pepper
sufficient cooked pasta to serve 4 people
freshly grated Parmesan cheese

———— • ————

1 Gently fry the onions in the oil for 10–12 minutes until they are very soft. Do not allow them to burn.

2 Add the courgettes and herbs. Cover and cook gently for a further 2–3 minutes. Season to taste.

3 Arrange the pasta on 4 plates and spoon the sauce over the top. Serve with plenty of freshly grated Parmesan.

Red Onions

These are really deep purple on the outside, with a shading of pink towards the centre. They fade a little as they are cooked but they do remain quite a pretty colour. They are on sale in autumn and winter.

SPRING SAUCE

Now that baby vegetables are so widely available in supermarkets you can recreate spring at any time of year. Many of these tender young vegetables come from France, so I decided to flavour this attractive sauce with French nut oil. It takes very little time to prepare if you keep the vegetables fairly chunky to match the pasta. Both penne and rigatoni work well.

———— • ————

10 new or baby carrots, halved lengthways
10 baby sweetcorn, halved lengthways
2 tablespoons peanut oil
1 tablespoon walnut or almond oil
1 small bunch spring onions, trimmed and cut into 6cm (2½in) lengths
8 baby courgettes, halved lengthways

50g (2oz) mangetout
50g (2oz) French beans, trimmed and cut into 6cm (2½in) lengths
1 tablespoon white wine vinegar
salt and freshly ground black pepper
sufficient cooked pasta to serve 4 people
freshly grated Parmesan cheese

———— • ————

1 Steam the carrots and baby sweetcorn in a very small amount of water for 3–4 minutes to soften a little.

2 Heat both oils in a wok or large frying pan. Then stir-fry the drained carrots and sweetcorn with the spring onion for 2 minutes.

3 Add the remaining vegetables and continue to stir-fry until they are as tender as you like them.

4 Sprinkle with the vinegar and seasoning, toss and spoon over the pasta. Serve with freshly grated Parmesan.

MANTUA SAUCE

In Mantua, pumpkin is used to stuff fresh ravioli. The filling is made by baking the whole pumpkin in the oven. The flesh is then scraped out and mixed with Amaretti biscuits and Mostardo di Cremona, a kind of spicy honey and fruit mixture. This is a similar but simpler mixture for use with short tubular pasta like penne or macaroni. Serve with a piquant rocket or watercress salad.

———————— • ————————

225g (8oz) peeled and seeded pumpkin flesh
50ml (2fl oz) sweet white wine
50ml (2fl oz) vegetable stock
25g (1oz) Amaretti biscuits, finely crushed (if pre-wrapped, 2 little packets will be sufficient)
1 teaspoon wholegrain mustard

40g (1¹/₂oz) freshly grated Parmesan cheese
salt and freshly ground black pepper
a pinch of grated nutmeg
4 tablespoons single cream
sufficient cooked pasta to serve 4 people as a starter

———————— • ————————

1 Place the pumpkin in a saucepan with the wine and bring to the boil. Simmer, covered, for 15 minutes until the pumpkin is very tender.

2 Mash with a wooden spoon and stir in all the remaining ingredients except the pasta. Continue cooking for another minute to heat through. Toss the pasta in the sauce and serve at once.

Amaretti Biscuits

These plump, crisp little biscuits are made with a mixture of sweet and bitter almonds and it is the latter which make them taste different to other macaroons. They are usually served with coffee but they also turn up in a number of savoury dishes such as this Mantua Sauce.

ITALIAN BEAN SAUCE

Almost every Italian province has its own bean-based sauce. This version comes from Tuscany. A very similar dish is served in the Veneto. The only difference is that the Tuscans use cannellini beans and the Venetians borlotti beans. The latter also tend to leave out the celery but I think the dish has a better flavour with it. Of course there is nothing to stop you experimenting with whatever beans you have to hand. Serve with penne or rigatoni and a salad of oak leaf lettuce.

——— • ———

4 tablespoons olive oil
1 clove garlic, peeled and finely chopped
2 sticks celery, trimmed and finely chopped
2 tablespoons freshly chopped parsley
leaves from 2 sprigs of fresh rosemary
4 firm tomatoes, seeded and diced

salt and freshly ground black pepper
1 × 400g (14oz) can cannellini or borlotti beans, drained, retaining 2 tablespoons juice
sufficient cooked pasta to serve 4 people
freshly grated Parmesan cheese

——— • ———

1 Heat the olive oil in a saucepan. Add the garlic, celery, parsley and rosemary and fry gently for 2 minutes.

2 Add the prepared tomatoes and seasoning and toss over the heat. Add the beans and the retained juice. Heat through carefully and spoon over the pasta. Serve with freshly grated Parmesan.

Variations

1 For a stronger flavour stir in 1 teaspoon sun-dried tomato paste (see page 21) or 1 tablespoon tomato purée just before serving.

2 Use tarragon in place of rosemary.

MEXICAN CHILLI SAUCE

This is an uncooked sauce inspired by the Mexican salsas or spicy relishes which are served with many of their main course dishes. The green chillis give it quite a kick and it goes well with rigatoni. The mixture can be gently warmed and served with hot pasta or it can be served cold as a pasta salad – very good for a cold buffet.

If you do not have time to chop everything finely you can toss it all into a food processor and blend it instead. The end result tastes just as good, although it does not look quite as interesting.

———— • ————

1 clove garlic, peeled and finely chopped
4–5 spring onions or 2 shallots, trimmed and finely chopped
1 fresh green chilli pepper, seeded and finely chopped
3 firm ripe tomatoes, seeded and chopped
1 small courgette, finely chopped

2 tablespoons freshly chopped coriander leaves
salt and freshly ground black pepper
juice of 1 lime or ½ lemon
4 tablespoons olive oil
sufficient cooked pasta to serve 4 people
a few sprigs of fresh coriander

———— • ————

1 Place all the ingredients, except the lime or lemon juice, oil, pasta and coriander sprigs, in a bowl.

2 Beat the lime or lemon juice and oil together and pour over the vegetables. Toss together and warm if required.

3 Mix the pasta with the sauce and serve, garnished with the sprigs of fresh coriander.

Variation

Add 1 × 200g (7oz) can drained and flaked tuna to the sauce to make a really substantial dish.

SAUCE NORMA

This aubergine and tomato sauce originated in Sicily long before Bellini discovered it but it has come to be named after his opera *Norma*. Some recipes call for spaghetti but I think the chunky pieces of aubergine go well with elbow macaroni. Finish the meal with an almond tart served with the island's own dessert wine – Marsala.

If you are short of time you could dispense with salting the aubergine. However you will then need to grill it, as it takes up too much oil if you fry it without prior salting.

———— • ————

1 large aubergine, sliced
salt
1 × 400g (14oz) can tomatoes
½ clove garlic, peeled and crushed
a pinch of sugar or salt

freshly ground black pepper
oil for frying
sufficient cooked pasta to serve 4 people
freshly grated Parmesan cheese

———— • ————

1 Place the sliced aubergine in a colander and sprinkle well with salt. Leave to stand for at least 30 minutes.

2 Put the tomatoes in a saucepan and add the garlic, sugar or salt, and black pepper. Bring to the boil, cover and cook over a medium heat for 10–15 minutes to reduce. Stir from time to time.

3 Wash, drain and dry the aubergine slices. Pour a good 2.5cm (1in) oil into a frying pan and fry the aubergines on both sides until golden.

4 Dice the aubergine and stir into the tomato sauce with 3 tablespoons freshly grated Parmesan.

5 Arrange the pasta on 4 plates and top with the sauce. Serve with more grated Parmesan and black pepper.

Variations

1 Add 4 tablespoons freshly chopped basil just before serving.

2 Add 1 heaped teaspoon anchovy pâté to the canned tomatoes at the start of the sauce. Omit the sugar or salt.

MOZZARELLA AND TOMATO SAUCE

The Mozzarella gives this sauce from Tuscany a thick stringy texture which goes well with short tubular pasta, particularly penne. It is delicious made with fresh tomatoes but if these are not available use 2 × 400g (14oz) drained cans of tomatoes. (Use the liquid for other sauces or soup.) Either way it is extremely quick to make.

Serve with a side salad of mixed leaves, finely shredded celery and chopped parsley.

———— • ————

3 tablespoons olive oil
1 fresh red chilli pepper, seeded and coarsely chopped
3 cloves garlic, peeled and finely chopped

450g (1lb) very ripe tomatoes, coarsely chopped
125g (4oz) Mozzarella cheese, cut into pieces
salt and freshly ground black pepper
sufficient cooked pasta to serve 4 people

———— • ————

1 Heat the oil in a large frying pan and gently fry the chilli and garlic for 1–2 minutes.

2 Add the tomatoes and cook over a fairly high heat for 5 minutes until most of the water from the tomatoes has evaporated.

3 Add the Mozzarella to the sauce. Lower the heat and stir until the cheese melts and combines with the tomatoes.

4 When the cheese begins to turn stringy add the pasta and seasoning and stir with a wooden spoon. The sauce should coat each piece of pasta. Serve in deep bowls, spooning any remaining sauce over the top.

Mozzarella Cheese

The best Mozzarella cheese was, and still is, made with buffalo milk. Some Italian grocers and delicatessens stock this type as well as cow's milk Mozzarella. Real Mozzarella has an irregular oval shape. It is packed in whey to keep it moist. Whatever you do, do not buy the rectangular-shaped Mozzarella. This does not come from Italy but from Denmark. It is often labelled 'Pizza Cheese'.

Manhattan Special

Like the Salmon with Nutmeg and Dill Sauce for long flat pasta (page 61), this sauce was inspired by the Silver Plate Restaurant in New York. The chunky strips of artichoke add an interesting texture to the basic tomato sauce and the chilli adds a touch of heat. It goes very well with most kinds of short tubular pasta.

It's a great standby if you have unexpected guests. All you have to do is raid the storecupboard! This quantity will serve 4 people as a starter, so double up if it is to be the main course or if you want to keep half in the fridge to make a cold pasta salad later in the week. It also freezes very successfully.

———— • ————

1 onion, peeled and finely chopped
1 clove garlic, peeled and finely chopped
1 tablespoon olive oil
1 × 400g (14 oz) can tomatoes, drained and chopped
1/4 teaspoon dried oregano
1 small dried red chilli pepper, crushed, and seeded or not, to taste

salt and freshly ground black pepper
1 × 297g (10 1/2oz) can artichoke bases, drained and cut into strips
2 tablespoons freshly chopped parsley
sufficient cooked pasta to serve 4 people as a starter
grated Pecorino Romano cheese

———— • ————

1 Gently fry the onion and garlic in the olive oil for 3–4 minutes until soft. Do not allow the mixture to turn brown.

2 Add the tomatoes, oregano, chilli pepper and seasoning and bring to the boil. Cook over a medium heat for 10 minutes.

3 Add the artichoke bases and parsley, heat through and spoon over the pasta. Serve with grated Pecorino.

GREEK SAUCE

This topping was inspired by those delicious Greek salads which are served at every meal in Athens and the Greek islands. The flavours are robust and fragrant and go well with tubular pasta. The secret is not to cook the vegetables for too long.

———— • ————

1 small onion or 6 spring onions, trimmed and coarsely chopped
3 tablespoons olive oil
4 firm ripe tomatoes, seeded and chopped
1 small cucumber, diced
20 black olives, stoned
2 sprigs fresh marjoram, chopped

leaves from 2 sprigs of fresh thyme or 1/2 teaspoon dried thyme
freshly ground black pepper
juice of 1/2 lemon
125g (4oz) Feta cheese, cut into small cubes
sufficient cooked pasta to serve 4 people

———— • ————

1 Fry the onion or spring onions in the oil for 1 minute only. Add the tomatoes, cucumber, olives, herbs and black pepper. Toss all together over a medium heat for another minute to warm through.

2 Add the lemon juice and bring to the boil. Stir in the cheese and cooked pasta. Toss and serve with more black pepper.

Variation

Instead of Feta try coarsely grated Halloumi cheese. The texture will not be quite so creamy but the flavour is good.

PEAS AND PASTA

Fresh peas pop up in a large number of different pasta dishes but they are often variations on the same theme. Here are some ideas from various parts of Italy and from nearer home.

PEAS AND PATERNOSTRI

This recipe comes from Puglia in the heel of Italy. It is a very simple dish based on fresh peas with small tubular pasta called paternostri. There is also an even smaller type called Avemarie. They are both named for two of the beads on a rosary. In other less religious parts of Italy these pastas are often known as ditalini. The local name for the dish is piselli e paternostri.

In Puglia, fresh rather than frozen peas are used. After shelling, the pods are boiled in a large pan of water for 10–15 minutes. The pods are then discarded and the water used to cook the pasta. The dish is unusual in that the peas are dominant and the pasta is secondary. It will serve 4 people, or 6 as a starter.

——————— • ———————

2 tablespoons olive oil
¹/₂ clove garlic, peeled and crushed
10 sprigs broadleaf parsley
450g (1lb) frozen peas

50ml (2fl oz) chicken or vegetable stock
sufficient cooked pasta to serve 4 people
salt and freshly ground black pepper

——————— • ———————

1 Heat the oil in a pan and fry the garlic for 2 minutes.

2 Strip the leaves from the parsley stalks and chop. Add to the garlic with the peas. Stir well and add the stock. Bring to the boil. Keep stirring and simmer for 2–3 minutes.

3 Add the pasta and toss over a medium heat for a further minute. Season, and serve sprinkled with more parsley.

PEAS WITH PANCETTA

Ham and peas are traditional partners in Italian soups and sauces, as they are elsewhere in Europe. This well-flavoured recipe comes from Central Italy. It is worth seeking out pancetta for the authentic flavour it gives. If you cannot find it unsmoked bacon can be used instead.

———— • ————

1 thick slice pancetta or 3 slices unsmoked streaky bacon, diced
2 tablespoons olive oil
1 clove garlic, peeled and chopped
1 onion, peeled and very finely chopped

350g (12oz) frozen peas
50ml (2fl oz) chicken or vegetable stock
salt and freshly ground black pepper
sufficient cooked pasta to serve 4 people
freshly grated Parmesan cheese

———— • ————

1 Fry the diced pancetta or bacon in the oil for 1 minute. Add the garlic and onion and continue frying for a further 3–4 minutes until they are soft but not brown.

2 Add the peas and stir well. Add the stock and bring to the boil. Simmer for 2 minutes and toss with the pasta. Serve with freshly grated Parmesan.

Variations

1 Add 225g (8oz) sliced mushrooms and some chopped parsley with the garlic and onion. Continue as above.

2 Add 225g (8oz) chicken livers, cut into chunks, after the garlic and onion and fry until just cooked before adding the peas.

PEAS WITH TOMATOES AND BASIL

A deliciously smoky aroma distinguishes this variation on the same theme from Tuscany. I came across the dish in a small restaurant in the red brick village of Poggi Bonzi in Central Tuscany and the proprietor agreed to give me an outline of the recipe. The rest was up to me.

———— • ————

2 slices smoked pancetta or 5 slices smoked streaky bacon, diced
2 tablespoons olive oil
1 small onion, peeled and finely chopped
1 clove garlic, peeled and crushed
1 × 400g (14oz) can tomatoes

salt and freshly ground black pepper
300g (10oz) frozen peas
leaves from 3 sprigs fresh basil, roughly chopped
sufficient cooked pasta to serve 4 people
a few sprigs of fresh basil

———— • ————

1 Fry the pancetta or bacon in the oil for 2 minutes. Add the onion and garlic and continue cooking for 3–4 minutes until the onion has softened. Do not allow the mixture to brown.

2 Add the contents of the can of tomatoes and seasonings and bring to the boil. Cover and cook over a medium heat for 10 minutes.

3 Add the peas and basil and return to the boil. Cook for a further 2–3 minutes. Toss with the pasta and serve at once, garnish with the sprigs of fresh basil.

SUMMER SAUCE

I call this Summer Sauce because it is best made with fresh garden peas and English tomatoes. However it can also be made with frozen peas. In this case boil the cream sauce for a further 1–2 minutes before adding the peas.

The sauce goes very well with any kind of tubular pasta. Serve with a salad of oakleaf lettuce and crusty wholemeal rolls.

———————— • ————————

2 tablespoons melted butter
2 tablespoons olive oil
8–10 spring onions, trimmed and roughly chopped
225g (8oz) small button mushrooms, wiped and halved or quartered
300ml (½ pint) double cream

4 tablespoons strong vegetable stock
salt and freshly ground black pepper
225g (8oz) peas
4 small firm English tomatoes, roughly chopped
sufficient cooked pasta to serve 4 people
freshly grated Parmesan cheese

———————— • ————————

1 Heat the butter and oil in a saucepan and gently fry the spring onions until soft. Add the mushrooms and cook for 2–3 minutes.

2 Add the cream, stock and seasoning and bring to the boil. Boil fast for 2–3 minutes.

3 Add the peas and continue cooking until the peas are tender and the sauce has thickened. Add the tomatoes. Return to the boil and cook for 1 minute before serving. Spoon over the pasta and serve with freshly grated Parmesan.

Variations

1 Use yoghurt instead of cream and stabilise with a little cornflour, or potato or rice flour.

2 Serve sprinkled with 2 tablespoons freshly chopped chervil.

PRAWN AND GREEN OLIVE SAUCE

Prawns abound in the fish markets of Provence and they are used in all kinds of dishes. The idea for this sauce came from a restaurant in Toulon where king prawns were served with very large pasta shells in a creamy sauce. I find the recipe works very well with ordinary peeled prawns and tubular pasta. Serve with a salad of young spinach leaves dressed in a light extra virgin olive oil (from Nyons or Les Baux if possible).

———— • ————

25g (1oz) butter
2 cloves garlic, peeled and crushed
grated rind of 1 lemon
4 tomatoes, seeded and chopped
12 green olives, stoned and quartered
150ml (¼ pint) double cream

3 tablespoons dry white wine
225g (8oz) peeled prawns
salt and freshly ground black pepper
3 tablespoons freshly chopped basil or
    tarragon
sufficient cooked pasta to serve 4 people

———— • ————

1 Melt the butter in a pan and fry the garlic and lemon rind for 1 minute. Add the tomatoes and olives and toss well.

2 Pour on the cream and wine and bring to the boil. Cook fairly fast for 5 minutes.

3 Toss in the prawns, seasoning and fresh basil or tarragon and heat through.

4 Pour the sauce over the pasta and serve with more black pepper.

PROSCUITTO AND MUSHROOM SAUCE

Whenever I see air-dried hams hanging up in the delicatessen I am reminded of the rows of hams I saw hanging in the sheds of Parma. Prosciutto and porcini mushrooms give an authentic Italian flavour to this sauce from the same area. You can substitute cultivated mushrooms and smoked ham for a milder but still very pleasant flavour.

Serve with a mixed leaf salad very lightly dressed with extra virgin olive oil and a good red wine vinegar. Garnish with shredded green peppers.

———————— • ————————

50g (2oz) dried porcini mushrooms
125g (4oz) prosciutto
125g (4oz) boiled ham
1 red onion, finely chopped
1 tablespoon butter
2 tablespoons olive oil
1 × 500ml (18fl oz) jar passato di pomodoro or 1 × 400g (14oz) can chopped tomatoes

100ml (4fl oz) double cream
salt and freshly ground black pepper
sufficient cooked pasta to serve 4 people
freshly grated Parmesan cheese

———————— • ————————

1 Barely cover the dried mushrooms with boiling water and leave to stand for 15–20 minutes. Drain, keeping the liquid for another dish.

2 Finely chop or mince the prosciutto with the ham and soaked mushrooms.

3 Gently fry the onion in the butter and oil for 2–3 minutes. Do not allow it to brown.

4 Add the meat mixture and the passata or chopped tomatoes and stir well.

5 Bring to the boil and cook, semi-covered, over a medium heat for 10–15 minutes to thicken the sauce.

6 Stir in the cream, reheat and season. Spoon over the pasta and serve with grated Parmesan.

PROSCIUTTO AND GOAT'S CHEESE SAUCE

Some traditional restaurants in Italy serve a set meal of dishes chosen daily by the chef as he shops in the local market. This sauce, served with thick penne, formed part of a gargantuan seven-course meal in just such a restaurant in the old part of Pescara on the Adriatic coast. The goat's cheese was the strongest flavour, so vegetarians could leave out the prosciutto and still have a tasty sauce. It makes an excellent supper dish served with a tomato and basil salad.

———— • ————

1 onion, peeled and finely chopped
2 tablespoons cooking oil
2 tablespoons dry white wine
2 tablespoons vegetable or chicken stock
175g (6oz) fresh well-flavoured goat's cheese, cut into small chunks

50g (2oz) prosciutto, finely diced
freshly ground black pepper
sufficient cooked pasta to serve 4 people
freshly grated hard goat's cheese or Pecorino Romano cheese

———— • ————

1 Gently fry the onion in the oil for 2–3 minutes until soft but not brown.

2 Add the wine and stock and stir in the cheese. When the cheese has melted completely stir in the prosciutto and black pepper and heat through.

3 Toss the cooked pasta in the sauce and serve with freshly ground black pepper and grated hard goat's cheese or Pecorino.

Prosciutto

This is the general name given to any kind of air-dried ham. In the UK the best-known variety is probably Parma ham. You can also buy San Danielle and prosciutto crudo. The latter is usually the cheapest as it does not come from a specific area.

ITALIAN SAUSAGE AND PEPPER SAUCE

Italian sausages are 100 per cent meat and have their own distinctive and very aromatic flavour. Traditional English sausages simply do not taste the same. Italian sausages can often be found in specialist delicatessen shops. They make a fairly heavy sauce which is good for tubular pasta such as rigatoni or the longer ziti.

———— • ————

6 small Italian sausages (about 225g
 (8oz) in total)
1 onion, peeled and finely chopped
1 tablespoon olive oil
1 large red pepper, seeded and cut into
 short strips
2 large ripe tomatoes, skinned, seeded
 and coarsely chopped

100ml (4fl oz) red wine
50ml (2fl oz) vegetable stock or water
a pinch of fennel seed
a pinch of dried oregano
a pinch of dried thyme
salt and freshly ground black pepper
sufficient cooked pasta to serve 4 people
 as a starter

———— • ————

1 Prick the sausages all over with a fork and place in a pan with 5mm (¼in) water. Bring to the boil and simmer for 20 minutes. When the pot runs dry, the sausages will begin to fry in their own fat. Cook for a further 10 minutes, turning occasionally. Drain on kitchen paper.

2 Meanwhile fry the onion in olive oil for 5–6 minutes until lightly browned. Add the red pepper and continue to fry for a further 2–3 minutes. Add all the remaining ingredients except the pasta. Bring to the boil and simmer fairly fast for 20 minutes. Add more stock if necessary.

3 Slice the sausages and mix with the sauce. Spoon onto the hot pasta and serve.

LIVORNESE SAUCE

This rich meat sauce comes from Leghorn on the Tuscan coast. There it is served with penne or rigatoni. If you prefer you could also serve it with spiral-shaped fusilli. Despite its meat base it does not take very long to cook. I usually chop the meat in a food processor but you do need to be careful not to over-process it. Serve with a crunchy salad of apples, celery and walnuts.

————— • —————

1 onion, peeled and finely chopped
2 cloves garlic, peeled and crushed
2 tablespoons olive oil
175g (6oz) gammon, finely chopped or minced
175g (6oz) lean pork, finely chopped or minced
a small bunch of fresh basil, roughly chopped

1/4 teaspoon dried thyme
1/4 teaspoon paprika
50ml (2fl oz) brandy
salt and freshly ground black pepper
sufficient cooked pasta to serve 4 people
freshly grated Parmesan cheese

————— • —————

1 Fry the onion and garlic in the oil for 3–4 minutes until soft.

2 Add the gammon and pork and seal all over.

3 Add all the remaining ingredients except the pasta and cheese and bring to the boil. Cover and simmer for 10 minutes.

4 Mix the pasta into the sauce and toss well together. Serve with freshly grated Parmesan.

Variation

Add 2–3 tablespoons frozen peas together with the brandy and other flavourings.

· CHAPTER FIVE ·

PASTA SHAPES

There is a whole host of different and sometimes intriguing pasta shapes on sale. Some are traditional shapes, others have been dreamt up by dried pasta manufacturers both here and in Italy.

Sauces with plenty of juice to fill pockets and interesting textures to match the pasta shapes are needed, but the simple sauces in Chapter 1 work well too.

All the types of pasta listed below are available dried but they can only rarely be bought fresh outside Italy. There are also wholemeal and flavoured versions of many of them.

For cooking instructions, see page xi.

CAVATIEDDI is a small mussel-shaped pasta from Apulia, usually hand-made.

CONCHIGLIE is shell-shaped. Smaller shells are known as *conchigliette*.

CORZETTI is a 'figure of eight' shape from Liguria.

FARFALLE is butterfly- or sometimes bow-shaped. It looks good with chunky sauces.

FUSILLI, or spiral-shaped pasta, comes in a variety of thicknesses.

ORECCHIETTE is known as 'little ears' in Italy and comes from Apulia. It takes longer to cook than some other shapes.

ROTELLE is a wheel-shaped pasta not widely found in Italy.

CAULIFLOWER AND SAFFRON SAUCE

The rich, vibrant colour of this Sicilian sauce comes from the saffron, and because this distinctively flavoured spice is so expensive it is usually only served on high days and holidays. I like to serve it with 'little ears' or orecchiette which is not a local choice, or fusilli which is. In Sicily the water-conscious locals use the water the cauliflower has been cooked in to cook the pasta.

——————— • ———————

1 small to medium-sized cauliflower
4 tablespoons olive oil
2 cloves garlic, peeled and crushed
1/4 teaspoon saffron strands or powder
3 firm tomatoes, seeded and coarsely chopped

1 tablespoon raisins or sultanas
1 tablespoon pine kernels, toasted (see page xi)
salt and freshly ground black pepper
sufficient cooked pasta to serve 4 people
freshly grated Pecorino Sardo cheese

——————— • ———————

1 Cover the cauliflower with boiling water and cook for 6–8 minutes. Drain, keeping the water to cook the pasta, and cut into florets. (I usually discard the stalks at this stage and keep them for soup but you can use them if you wish.)

2 Heath the oil in a pan and fry the garlic and saffron for 1 minute. Add the cauliflower florets and stir-fry until the cauliflower is almost tender.

3 Add the tomatoes, raisins or sultanas, pine kernels, seasoning and 3 tablespoons cauliflower water. Continue to stir-fry for another 1–2 minutes to heat through.

4 Toss the pasta with the sauce and serve with the grated Pecorino Sardo.

GREEN BEAN AND POTATO SAUCE

The idea of serving potatoes with pasta is rather surprising but it is authentic. It comes from the mountains of Northern Italy and makes a very warming and filling dish – exactly what you need on a winter's day after a long walk in the snowy foothills of the Alps. Start with a bowl of home-made soup and finish with some almond biscuits and a bottle of Trentino Vin Santo. Fusilli works well in this dish.

———— • ————

450g (1lb) small new potatoes, scrubbed and quartered
a pinch of salt
225g (8oz) uncooked dried pasta
350g (12oz) green beans, trimmed and sliced
50g (2oz) butter

15–16 large leaves fresh sage, each torn into 2–3 pieces
175g (6oz) Pecorino Fresco or Caerphilly cheese, diced
2 tablespoons freshly grated Parmesan cheese
freshly ground black pepper

———— • ————

1 Cover the potatoes in plenty of boiling salted water and cook for 5 minutes.

2 Add the pasta and beans and return to the boil. Simmer for 10–12 minutes until both the pasta and potatoes are cooked and the beans are tender.

3 Drain well and toss with all the remaining ingredients. Serve with more freshly ground black pepper.

BLUE CHEESE AND BROCCOLI SAUCE

Broccoli and blue cheese blend well with pasta. Choose a mild and creamy cheese, as the heat brings out the flavour and a cheese like Gorgonzola would probably be too overpowering. The dish looks particularly attractive if you use spinach- and tomato-flavoured spirals mixed with plain fusilli.

The faster you cook the broccoli, the better the texture and the quicker you will get your meal! Serve with a grated carrot and celery salad.

———— • ————

225g (8oz) broccoli or calabrese
1 tablespoon olive oil
1 small onion, peeled and finely chopped
150ml (¼ pint) dry white wine
4 tablespoons double cream

125g (4oz) mild blue cheese such as Blue
  Brie, Cambozola or Dolcelatte
freshly ground black pepper
sufficient cooked pasta to serve 4 people
a few sprigs of broadleaf parsley

———— • ————

1 Cook the broccoli or calabrese in lightly salted, boiling water for 6–7 minutes until just cooked, but still slightly crisp. Drain and cut into small florets, and the stems into pieces.

2 Heat the oil in a pan and gently fry the onion for 2–3 minutes until soft. Add the white wine and cream and bring to the boil. Cut the cheese into small chunks and stir into the sauce with the seasonings.

3 Toss the broccoli or calabrese with the pasta and pour the sauce on top. Garnish with the sprigs of parsley and serve at once.

CHICKPEAS WITH OIL AND FLAVOURINGS

One of the simplest pasta sauces I have come across is a traditional dish from Basilica in Southern Italy. The chickpeas are dressed with clove-flavoured onions and served with farfalle. Recipes from other areas use tomato sauce, prosciutto and rocket.

CHICKPEAS WITH ONIONS AND CLOVES

This is a slightly more elaborate version of the Basilican dish. Use canned chickpeas for speed but discard the liquid from the can.

––––––––– • –––––––––

4 tablespoons extra virgin olive oil
3 cloves
2 large onions, peeled and sliced
$\frac{1}{2}$ × 400g (14oz) can chickpeas, drained
3 tablespoons well-flavoured vegetable or chicken stock

salt and freshly ground black pepper
1 teaspoon tomato purée (optional)
sufficient cooked pasta to serve 4 people
freshly grated Parmesan cheese

––––––––– • –––––––––

1 Heat the oil in a large pan and fry the cloves for 1 minute. Add the onions and continue frying until lightly browned. Remove the cloves.

2 Stir in the chickpeas and stock and continue cooking for a further minute. Season to taste, adding a little tomato purée if desired.

3 Toss with the pasta and serve with freshly grated Parmesan.

CHICKPEAS WITH PROSCIUTTO AND ROCKET

The bitter flavour of the rocket complements that of the chickpeas in this classic from the city of Potenza in the Southern Appenines. When I ate there, gnarled olive trees clung to the hillsides below the restaurant terrace and the air was full of the scent of the proprietor's herb garden.

————— • —————

4 tablespoons extra virgin olive oil
3 tablespoons freshly chopped parsley
a handful of coarsely chopped rocket
1 tablespoon freshly chopped tarragon
a little grated lemon rind

50g (2oz) prosciutto, diced
½ × 400g (14oz) can chickpeas, drained
sufficient cooked pasta to serve 4 people
freshly ground black pepper
freshly grated Parmesan cheese

————— • —————

1 Heat the oil in a large saucepan and fry the fresh herbs and lemon rind for 1 minute. Add the prosciutto and chickpeas and mix well.

2 Add the pasta and black pepper and toss together. Serve with freshly grated Parmesan.

TURKISH TAHINA SAUCE

This Turkish sauce is usually served on baked fish or steamed vegetables such as beans or cauliflower. However I have adapted it to serve with pasta shapes with great results. A green salad completes the meal.

———— • ————

125g (4oz) shelled walnuts
1 clove garlic
¹/₂ teaspoon salt
4 tablespoons tahina

juice of 2 lemons
4 tablespoons freshly chopped parsley
sufficient cooked pasta to serve 4 people

———— • ————

1 Place all the ingredients except the pasta in a blender or food processor with 5–6 tablespoons water and blend until you get a good consistency. Do not blend too much or you will lose the slightly rough texture provided by the walnuts.

2 Transfer to a saucepan and heat gently, adding more water as the mixture starts to thicken. Do not allow the sauce to boil.

3 Toss the pasta in the sauce and serve at once.

Tahina

This paste is made all over the Middle East and simply consists of ground sesame seeds. It is possible to make it at home but it is quicker and easier to use a jar of ready-made tahina, available from delicatessens and some supermarkets.

COURGETTE AND GARLIC SAUCE

There are lots of courgette or zucchini recipes but I think this one is the best. The flavours of the onion, garlic and courgette blend beautifully and the basil sets it all off well. Serve with any kind of pasta shape.

———— • ————

2 onions, peeled and sliced
2 cloves garlic, peeled and crushed
50g (2oz) butter
1 tablespoon olive oil
350g (12oz) courgettes, cubed

salt and freshly ground black pepper
10 basil leaves, torn into pieces
sufficient cooked pasta to serve 4 people
freshly grated Parmesan cheese

———— • ————

1 Gently fry the onion and garlic in the butter and oil. Do not allow them to burn.

2 After 3–4 minutes add the courgettes and seasonings and continue cooking gently until the courgettes are just cooked. This will take 15–20 minutes, depending on the size of the cubes.

3 Add the basil leaves and the pasta. Toss well and serve with a knob of butter on top of each plate and plenty of freshly grated Parmesan.

SICILIAN AUBERGINE SAUCE

Aubergines are a great favourite in Sicily and no market is complete without great mounds of this beautifully shiny, deep purple vegetable. They crop up in lots of sauces with all kinds of different ingredients and flavourings. Here toasted nuts and seeds give a slightly crunchy texture.

I think this particular sauce goes well with rotelle, the pasta shaped like small wheels. Serve with a mixed leaf salad, including rocket or watercress, dressed with goat's milk yoghurt and lemon juice.

———— • ————

1 tablespoon pine kernels
1 tablespoon sunflower seeds
2 cloves garlic, peeled and crushed
5 tablespoons olive oil
1½ tablespoons sun-dried tomato paste (see page 21)
1 large aubergine, diced

4 tomatoes, coarsely chopped
4 tablespoons freshly chopped parsley
salt and freshly ground black pepper
sufficient cooked pasta to serve 4 people
8–12 black olives
a few sprigs of fresh broadleaf parsley

———— • ————

1 Toast the pine kernels and sunflower seeds under the grill or in a dry frying pan.

2 Fry the garlic in the oil and add the sun-dried tomato paste. Stir and add the aubergine. Cook gently over a low heat for 8–12 minutes until just tender (do not allow to go mushy).

3 Add the fresh tomatoes, chopped parsley, toasted nuts and seeds, and seasonings and cook for a further 2–3 minutes.

4 Spoon over the pasta and garnish with the black olives and sprigs of fresh parsley.

PUGLIAN CAULIFLOWER SAUCE

This is one of the many vegetable sauces served as a starter with Puglia's famous 'little ears' pasta or orecchiette. They are not often made at home now but I have seen women making them by hand in the back streets of Bari and Brindisi on the Adriatic. In this part of Italy people like a piquant flavour and the hot pepper flakes would certainly be used.

———————— • ————————

1 small cauliflower or 1/2 large one
salt
2 whole cloves garlic, peeled
5 anchovy fillets in oil, drained, or 2 teaspoons anchovy pâté (see page 33)
3 tablespoons olive oil
sufficient cooked pasta to serve 4 people as a starter

freshly ground black pepper
leaves from 10 large sprigs broadleaf parsley
1/2 teaspoon hot red pepper flakes or chilli oil, (see page 100) (optional)

———————— • ————————

1 Cut the cauliflower into florets and discard the stalks. Put the florets into boiling salted water with the garlic and boil fast for 1 minute. Drain the cooking liquid into another pan and use to cook the orecchiette. Discard the garlic and keep the cauliflower warm.

2 Fry the anchovy fillets in the olive oil until they disintegrate. Toss the cooked pasta in this paste, or the anchovy pâté, if using. Add the cauliflower, check the seasoning and toss over a low heat for 1 minute.

3 Sprinkle with the parsley leaves and red pepper flakes or chilli oil and serve at once.

Variations

1 Use broccoli or calabrese in place of cauliflower and top with toasted pine kernels rather than parsley.

2 In Puglia turnip tops are often used in place of cauliflower or broccoli. These are not easily available here but Swiss chard makes a good substitute. Slice the stalks and toss with the water first, adding the leaves for 1 minute only.

RICH RICOTTA SAUCE

The classic version of this sauce, which was first cooked for me by a friend who lives in Rome, is made with a mild ewe's milk ricotta. However I have made it with the more strongly flavoured goat's milk ricotta and with fresh goat's cheese. Other cheeses which work well include garlic and herb roulades or Boursin.

The sauce is quite thick but still manages to get into the hollows and folds of most pasta shapes. Serve with a raw spinach salad.

———— • ————

1/2 quantity Simple Tomato Sauce from
Naples (see page 22)
150ml (1/4 pint) double cream
125g (4oz) ricotta or fresh goat's cheese,
slightly mashed

freshly ground black pepper
sufficient cooked pasta to serve 4 people
freshly grated Parmesan cheese

———— • ————

1 Heat the Tomato Sauce in a pan and stir in the cream. Bring the mixture almost to the boil.

2 Add the cheese and black pepper and heat through. Pour over the pasta and toss well together.

3 Serve with freshly grated Parmesan cheese.

Variation

Add freshly chopped herbs just before serving.

ROCKET SAUCE

The Italians like the pungent flavour of rocket and, as well as adding it to salads, use it to great effect with pasta. Mixed with a really sharp and full-flavoured cheese like Pecorino Romano, it makes a very interesting sauce base. There is not much cooking involved either!

If I am entertaining mid-week, I often serve this dish as a main course, starting with a plate of prosciutto and melon and finishing with Tiramisu.

———— • ————

5 tablespoons extra virgin olive oil
2 cloves garlic, peeled and crushed
1–2 small whole dried red chillies

sufficient cooked pasta to serve 4 people
50g (2oz) rocket, roughly torn
freshly grated Pecorino Romano cheese

———— • ————

1 Heat the olive oil in a large frying pan and fry the garlic and chilli for 1–2 minutes until brown.

2 Add the pasta to the pan with the rocket. Quickly toss all the ingredients together and serve with freshly grated Pecorino.

Pecorino Cheese

Pecorino cheese is the general name for ewe's milk cheese made in Central and Southern Italy. Each area produces cheese with its own characteristics. Pecorino Romano is aged for eight months. It is hard, salty and very piquant and is best used for grating. Pecorino Tuscano is almost always eaten when it is young and soft. Pecorino Sardo can be eaten when it is still quite young and fresh but it will harden and gain in piquancy with maturity. Young Pecorino is known as Pecorino Fresco.

ROCKET AND TOMATO SAUCE

If you are not sure about the flavour of rocket try boiling it with the pasta. It is not nearly as pungent cooked in this way but it does look very attractive with pasta bows or shells. The tomato sauce will supply the flavour, and make sure you have plenty of freshly grated grana cheese, which is similar to Parmesan.

———— • ————

125g (4oz) rocket
a pinch of salt
1 teaspoon olive oil
225g–350g (8–12 oz) uncooked dried
  pasta

1 quantity Classic Tomato Sauce (page
  24)
freshly grated grana cheese

———— • ————

1 Place the rocket in a large pan filled with water. Bring to the boil and add the salt, olive oil and pasta. Cook as directed on the pack.

2 Make the Tomato Sauce or reheat from the fridge or freezer.

3 Drain the pasta and rocket and spoon onto 4 plates. Top with the Tomato Sauce and serve with freshly grated grana cheese.

Variation

Sorrel could be used in place of rocket in both these recipes and Swiss chard leaves could be used in Rocket Sauce, though it would probably be too limp for Rocket and Tomato Sauce.

BEAN AND ONION SAUCE

This recipe comes from Puglia where it would most commonly be served with home-made orecchiette or cavatieddi. The latter are rather like little shells.

——————— • ———————

1 × 400g (14oz) can cannellini or hari-
  cot beans, drained
4 tablespoons olive oil
2 cloves garlic, peeled and cut in half
3 whole dried red chilli peppers
2 bayleaves
2 red onions, peeled and sliced

3 small stalks celery, trimmed and
  sliced, or ½ teaspoon celery salt
2 tablespoons white or red wine
3–4 tablespoons vegetable stock or water
salt and freshly ground black pepper
sufficient cooked pasta to serve 4 people
a little chilli oil

——————— • ———————

1 Purée the beans in a food processor or rub through a sieve.

2 Heat the oil in a pan and fry the garlic, chillies and bayleaves until well browned. Remove from the oil with a slotted spoon.

3 Fry the onions and celery or celery salt in the flavoured oil for 4–5 minutes until golden. Add the bean purée, wine, stock or water, and seasonings and bring to the boil.

4 Spoon over the pasta and serve with a little chilli oil.

Chilli Oil

Very spicy flavours are popular in Southern Italy and most cooks will have a special chilli oil to hand. This can be bought or made at home by steeping 2–3 dried red chilli peppers in a jar of olive oil for 2–3 weeks.

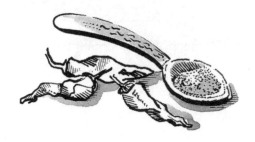

ITALIAN CRUNCHY SAUCE

I first tried this mixture as a stuffing for grilled vegetables and liked it so much that I looked for other ways of using the same combination of flavours. Pasta was the answer. The mixture of distinctively flavoured ingredients makes a wonderful sauce. It also retains much of its bite to give an interesting crunchy texture. I often serve this sauce as a starter with spirals but you could use bows or wheels.

———— • ————

2 tablespoons sultanas or raisins
2 tablespoons capers
2 tablespoons pine kernels
24 black olives, stoned and quartered
1/2 clove garlic, peeled and crushed
6 small spring onions, trimmed and chopped

freshly ground black pepper
6–8 tablespoons extra virgin olive oil
sufficient cooked pasta to serve 4 people as a starter
2 tablespoons freshly chopped parsley

———— • ————

1 Place the sultanas or raisins in a cup with the capers and cover with water. Leave to stand for 10–15 minutes, changing water once.

2 Toast the pine kernels under the grill until they turn golden.

3 Drain the caper mixture and chop with the pine kernels and olives or process coarsely in a food processor.

4 Mix in the garlic, spring onions, black pepper and 4–6 tablespoons oil (retaining 2 tablespoons). Spoon into a small shallow heatproof dish, place under the grill and cook for 3–4 minutes, stirring from time to time.

5 Toss the pasta in the remaining oil and add the vegetable mixture. Toss again and serve sprinkled with the chopped parsely and more black pepper.

Variation

Add 3–4 chopped anchovy fillets to the mixture.

COLD SEAFOOD AND BASIL SAUCE

This American recipe for shell pasta is perfect served on a bed of lettuce on summer evenings. It can be eaten warm or at room temperature. The original recipe specifies shrimps, scallops and squid but any mixture of ready-prepared shellfish can be used. Failing this, use cooked prawns alone.

———— • ————

225g (8oz) mixed cooked shellfish, seasoned with a little salt
sufficient cooked pasta to serve 4 people
1 small red pepper, seeded and diced
½ bunch spring onions, trimmed and chopped
75g (3oz) cooked petit pois

3 tablespoons freshly chopped basil
2 tablespoons freshly chopped parsley
a pinch of dried thyme or oregano
6 tablespoons olive oil
1 tablespoon lemon juice
salt and freshly ground black pepper
1 tablespoon capers, drained

———— • ————

1 Toss the shellfish and pasta together with the red peppers, spring onions and peas. If you prefer to serve the dish warm do this as soon as the pasta is cooked and drained.

2 Beat together the herbs, olive oil, lemon juice and seasoning. Heat gently in a pan if serving warm, but do not allow the mixture to get too hot. Pour over the pasta mixture.

3 Spoon onto 4 plates and sprinkle with the capers and more black pepper. Serve at once.

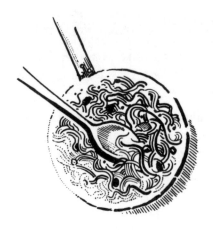

SALMON AND WALNUT SAUCE

Even though salmon is not a native of the Mediterranean it often appears on Italian menus. This sauce comes from a restaurant perched on a rocky promontory just outside San Remo on the Italian Riviera. We sat in the sunshine looking out over the sea and downing a glass of the local fizz. The sauce was served with corzetti, a local pasta shape, but it is just as good with fusilli.

———— • ————

350g (12oz) fresh salmon steak
3 tablespoons olive oil
1 onion, peeled and sliced
75ml (3fl oz) white wine
3 tablespoons tomato purée

salt and freshly ground black pepper
1 tablespoon freshly chopped basil or parsley
8 walnut halves, finely chopped
sufficient cooked pasta to serve 4 people

———— • ————

1 Skin the fish and cut away from the bones. Boil the bones with a little water to make some fish stock. Cut the fish into thin strips.

2 Heat the oil in a pan and fry the onion for 2–3 minutes until soft but not brown. Add the fish and cook for a further 5 minutes, stirring all the time.

3 Now add the wine, 75ml (3fl oz) of fish stock, tomato purée and seasonings and bring to the boil. Simmer for another 5 minutes.

4 Add half the basil or parsley and half the walnuts. Blend in a food processor until smooth.

5 Reheat and stir in the pasta and the remaining basil or parsley and walnuts. Toss well together and serve with more black pepper.

Variation

You can use canned salmon or tuna in place of fresh fish. In fact canned tuna works rather better than canned salmon, though of course the flavour is different.

MONKFISH AND TOMATO SAUCE

Choose quite a large size of conchiglie for this dish so that the sauce can gather in delicious pools inside the pasta shells. Cut the pieces of monkfish to about the same size so that the dish is quite chunky in appearance.

For a really quick sauce I use bottled Passato di Pomodoro. You can use a good-quality canned tomato juice instead but the sauce will need to be boiled for longer to achieve the correct consistency and you may need to use more.

———————— • ————————

2 cloves garlic, peeled and chopped
1 onion, peeled and finely chopped
2 tablespoons olive oil
1 × 680 (1½lb) bottle passato di pomodoro or can of tomato juice
2 teaspoons tomato purée
150ml (¼ pint) dry white wine or fish stock

salt and freshly ground black pepper
4 small monkfish tails, skinned and cut into 8 fillets (the fishmonger will do this for you)
sufficient cooked pasta to serve 4 people
4–6 sprigs fresh basil

———————— • ————————

1 Gently fry the garlic and onion in the oil until soft but not brown.

2 Pour on the passato or tomato juice and stir in the tomato purée, wine or stock and seasonings. Bring to the boil and simmer for 5–6 minutes until the sauce has thickened.

3 Cut the monkfish fillets into chunks and add to the sauce. Cook for a further 4–6 minutes until the fish is cooked through. Take care not to overcook or the fish will go hard.

4 Pour over the pasta and toss gently to allow the sauce to penetrate the shells.

5 Dot with the sprigs of basil and serve at once.

FLORENTINE SAUCE WITH GREEN PEPPERCORNS

Dishes cooked with spinach are often described as 'Florentine' because the citizens of Florence have always had a predeliction for this vegetable. However this colourful pasta sauce comes from my Roman friend's repertoire and she is not sure where it originally came from!

It looks very pretty with bows, butterflies or wheels but it is vital to add the spinach at the last minute, or it will go limp.

———— • ————

125g (4oz) salami
125g (4oz) smoked ham
sufficient cooked pasta to serve 4 people
2 tablespoons olive oil

125g (4oz) spinach or Swiss chard leaves, shredded
2 tablespoons green peppercorns
freshly ground black pepper
freshly grated Parmesan cheese

———— • ————

1 Skin and dice the salami and cut the ham into small thin strips.

2 Add to the pasta and toss over a low heat to warm through thoroughly.

3 Add the oil, spinach or Swiss chard, green peppercorns and black pepper and serve at once with freshly grated Parmesan.

Swiss Chard

This green vegetable has large flat leaves which taste very like spinach. The stalks are much thicker and more pronounced and can be sliced and cooked as a vegetable in their own right. If they are to be served with the leaves they will need a slightly longer cooking time.

WILD MUSHROOM AND PANCETTA SAUCE

The flavour of this sauce is punchy and robust. I usually serve it with fusilli. You do not need a great deal to flavour a bowlful so don't worry if you think there isn't all that much! Serve with sliced cucumber which has been marinated in a light vinegar dressing.

———— • ————

35–50g (1½–2oz) dried mixed wild mushrooms

2 heaped tablespoons tomato purée

2 heaped teaspoons sun-dried tomato paste (see page 21)

2 thick slices pancetta or unsmoked bacon (about 175g/6oz)

1 onion, peeled and finely chopped

2 cloves garlic, peeled and crushed

salt and freshly ground black pepper

sufficient cooked pasta to serve 4 people

———— • ————

1 Place the mushrooms in a bowl and just cover with boiling water. Leave to stand for 20 minutes.

2 Drain, keeping the liquid, and chop. Mix the liquid with the tomato purée and paste.

3 Fry the rind and fat from the pancetta in a small pan to render the fat. Chop the remaining meat into small cubes.

4 Remove the bits of rind from the pan and fry the onion and garlic in the fat until golden. Add the lean diced pancetta and fry for a further minute. Add the chopped mushrooms, the tomato paste mixture and seasonings.

5 Bring to the boil and cook over a medium heat for about 5 minutes until the sauce is fairly thick. Stir from time to time.

6 Spoon over the pasta, toss and serve.

HARLEQUIN PASTA

The colourful mixture of red peppers, sweetcorn and peas inspired the name of this dish. It looks very colourful and attractive and is fun to serve if you are entertaining friends. Butterfly or bow shapes are the prettiest choice. For the best results, keep the meatballs very small so they do not dwarf the pasta shapes.

350g (12oz) leg or shoulder of lamb steaks, minced
1 teaspoon freshly chopped mint
1 tablespoon freshly chopped parsley
a pinch of chilli powder or cayenne pepper
salt and freshly ground black pepper
2 tablespoons olive oil

1 clove garlic, peeled and crushed
1 × 400g (14oz) can chopped tomatoes, drained
1 small red pepper, seeded and diced
50g (2oz) frozen peas
50g (2oz) frozen sweetcorn kernels
sufficient cooked pasta to serve 4 people
a few sprigs of mint

1 Mix the minced lamb with the mint, parsley, chilli powder or cayenne, salt and pepper. Shape into tiny balls.

2 Heat 1 tablespoon olive oil in a frying pan over a high heat. Add the meatballs and fry until browned. Reduce the heat and fry for a further 2–3 minutes.

3 In a saucepan, mix the garlic, tomatoes and remaining olive oil and simmer gently for 5 minutes.

4 Add the red pepper, peas and sweetcorn and continue cooking for 5–6 minutes until the vegetables are just tender.

5 Toss all the ingredients together with the pasta and serve garnished with the sprigs of mint.

CHICKEN LIVER SAUCE

This punchy sauce goes particularly well with orecchiette or 'little ears'. It is quite rich and a little goes a long way. It makes a good special occasion first course. Follow with veal or pork medallions in lemon and butter sauce with green beans and a salad.

———— • ————

25g (1oz) butter
½ onion, peeled and finely chopped
3 tablespoons freshly chopped parsley
225g (8oz) chicken livers, roughly chopped
1 teaspoon flour
2 tablespoons Vin Santo or sweet white wine

salt and freshly ground black pepper
150ml (¼ pint) double cream
sufficient cooked pasta to serve 4 people as a starter
freshly grated Parmesan cheese

———— • ————

1 Melt the butter in a pan and add the onion, parsley and chicken livers. Gently fry for 3–4 minutes.

2 Sprinkle with the flour, stir well and add the wine and seasonings. Cook over a low heat for 2 minutes and add the cream. Bring the mixture to the boil and simmer for a further 5 minutes.

3 Spoon over the pasta and serve with freshly grated Parmesan.

Vin Santo

Vin Santo is a very rich, highly aromatic wine which is produced mainly in the Trentino and Tuscany. It is made from grapes which have been dried in the sun and is usually fairly sweet.

LIGURIAN VEAL SAUCE

Some people are unhappy about the way calves are treated on Dutch farms. The laws here are a little more humane and so I always try to buy English veal. However, if you do not want to use veal at all, pork can be substituted very successfully. The sauce works well with most shapes but I particularly like to serve it with rotelle or wheels.

———————— • ————————

25g (1oz) dried mixed wild mushrooms
1 onion, peeled and finely chopped
1 clove garlic, peeled and crushed
3 tablespoons olive oil
350g (12oz) minced veal or pork
2 tablespoons freshly chopped parsley
1 tablespoon freshly chopped sage or
* 1 teaspoon dried sage*

a little grated lemon rind
4 tablespoons red wine
1–2 tablespoons capers
1 teaspoon cornflour
sufficient cooked pasta to serve 4 people
freshly grated Parmesan cheese

———————— • ————————

1 Pour a little boiling water over the mushrooms and leave to stand for 15 minutes. Drain, keeping the liquid, and chop.

2 Meanwhile fry the onion and garlic in the oil until lightly browned. Add the meat and seal all over.

3 Add the parsley, sage, lemon rind, wine and capers and bring to the boil. Add the chopped mushrooms and simmer for 15 minutes.

4 Mix the mushroom liquor with the cornflour and add to the sauce. Return to the boil and cook for a further 5–6 minutes.

5 Pour the sauce over the pasta and serve with the freshly grated Parmesan.

SESAME CHICKEN SAUCE

I find it very surprising that the Italians rarely use chicken in their pasta sauces. Contrast this with the Far East where chicken appears to great effect in a good many noodle dishes. In this 'East meets West' sauce I have taken the best elements of the two approaches to make what has become one of my favourite supper dishes. I usually use farfalle and serve a salad of freshly sliced raw mangetout with lollo rosso dressed with a simple vinaigrette.

———— • ————

3 tablespoons sesame seeds
2 tablespoons cornflour
salt and freshly ground black pepper
3 small chicken breast fillets, skinned and cut into strips or 4 boned and skinned chicken thighs, cut into strips
3 tablespoons peanut or corn oil
1 teaspoon roasted sesame oil
1 tablespoon soy sauce

1 bunch spring onions, trimmed and cut into lengths
coarsely grated rind and juice of 2 tangerines or satsumas
50ml (2fl oz) Amontillado sherry
50ml (2fl oz) chicken stock
sufficient cooked pasta to serve 4 people
sprigs of broadleaf parsley

———— • ————

1 Gently fry the sesame seeds in a dry frying pan until they are well toasted but not burnt.

2 Mix the toasted sesame seeds with the cornflour and seasonings. Toss the strips of chicken in this mixture so that they are well coated. Keep any remaining mix to thicken the sauce at the end of the cooking time.

3 Heat the two oils in a wok or large deep frying pan and fry the spring onion and tangerine peel for 1 minute. Add the coated strips of chicken and stir fry over a medium heat until they are cooked through. This will take about 2–3 minutes depending on the thickness of the strips. Cut a piece of chicken in half to check that there is no pinkness showing.

4 Add all the remaining ingredients to the wok or pan, including the tangerine juice and any left-over coating mix. Stir and bring to the boil. Cook for a further two minutes.

5 Drain the cooked pasta and arrange on four plates. Top with the chicken mixture, spooning any excess sauce over each plate. Garnish with a few small sprigs of fresh broadleaf parsley. Serve at once.

Variation

If you cannot get tangerines or satsumas use clementines or oranges.

PANCETTA AND BEAN SAUCE

Like so many of the best pasta suaces there are only a few ingredients in this simple sauce from Liguria. The secret of its success lies in the unique combination of flavours and it took me quite a lot of experimenting to get it right. It is important to use the pretty pale green beans which are sold as flageolet beans in the UK. White cannellini beans just do not have the same flavour. Serve with fusilli.

———————— • ————————

175g (6oz) smoked pancetta
2 tablespoons extra virgin olive oil
½ teaspoon fennel seeds
4 small courgettes, trimmed and diced
1 × 398g (14oz) can flageolet beans,
  drained and wash in cold water

100ml (4fl oz) double cream
salt and freshly ground black pepper
sufficient cooked pasta to serve 4 people

———————— • ————————

1 Remove any excess fat from the pancetta and place these pieces of fat in a large saucepan. Heat gently to release the fat. Remove the pieces from the pan before continuing with the recipe.

2 Cut the remaining pancetta into very small dice. Add the oil to the fat in the saucepan and fry the pancetta until lightly browned. Add the fennel seeds and fry for another minute or so. Next add the courgettes and toss with the pancetta and fennel seeds over a medium heat for about 3–4 minutes.

3 Add the cream and seasonings. Bring to the boil. Make sure that the beans are well drained and add to the pan. Cook for a further 1–2 minutes to heat the beans through. Take care not to break them up when stirring.

4 Drain the pasta and toss with the sauce. Serve at once.

CALIFORNIAN PORK SAUCE

This recipe was inspired by the unusual flavour combinations used by the American chef of a nearby restaurant. He comes from California and is not restricted by the usual European traditions. He is quite happy to mix Scandinavian flavours with those of Thailand, or Caribbean ingredients with those of central Europe. So this is my attempt at a completely cosmopolitan sauce!

Serve it with fusilli, rotelle or conchiglie. I usually opt for the latter as the thick sauce collects in the cavities rather well.

———————— • ————————

3 tablespoons peanut or corn oil
350g (12oz) lean pork steaks, trimmed and cut into small dice
1 × 400g (14oz) can tomatoes
1 bunch spring onions, very finely chopped or minced
1 red pepper, seeded and very finely chopped or minced

1 × 2½cm (1 inch) piece fresh root ginger, peeled and grated
2 cloves garlic, peeled and crushed
grated rind and juice of 1 lime
salt and freshly ground black pepper
25g (1oz) fresh coriander, chopped but retaining 8–12 sprigs for garnish
sufficient cooked pasta for 4 people
2 tablespoons toasted peanuts

———————— • ————————

1 Heat the oil in a large pan and fry the pork until it is lightly browned all over.

2 Add the contents of the can of tomatoes and all the remaining ingredients except the coriander, the pasta and the peanuts. Bring the mixture to the boil and cook over a medium heat for 15 minutes, stirring from time to time.

3 Add the chopped coriander and continue cooking for a further 5 minutes.

4 Drain the pasta and toss with the sauce, making sure that it is well coated. Serve garnished with the reserved sprigs of coriander and the toasted peanuts.

INDEX